ENDGIN

ELLE HARKER

Trilogy Christian Publishers

A Wholly Owned Subsidiary of Trinity Broadcasting Network

2442 Michelle Drive

Tustin, CA 92780

Copyright © 2024 by Elle Harker

Unless otherwise indicated, all Scripture quotations are taken from the Holy Bible, New International Version®, NIV®. Copyright © 1973, 1978, 1984, 2011 by Biblica, Inc.TM Used by permission of Zondervan. All rights reserved worldwide. www.zondervan.com. The "NIV" and "New International Version" are trademarks registered in the United States Patent and Trademark Office by Biblica, Inc.TM. Scripture quotations marked KJV are taken from the King James Version of the Bible. Public domain.

All rights reserved, including the right to reproduce this book or portions thereof in any form whatsoever.

For information, address Trilogy Christian Publishing

Rights Department, 2442 Michelle Drive, Tustin, Ca 92780.

Trilogy Christian Publishing/ TBN and colophon are trademarks of Trinity Broadcasting Network.

For information about special discounts for bulk purchases, please contact Trilogy Christian Publishing.

Trilogy Disclaimer: The views and content expressed in this book are those of the author and may not necessarily reflect the views and doctrine of Trilogy Christian Publishing or the Trinity Broadcasting Network.

10 9 8 7 6 5 4 3 2 1

Library of Congress Cataloging-in-Publication Data is available.

ISBN 979-8-89333-325-1

ISBN 979-8-89333-326-8 (ebook)

DEDICATION

I would like to dedicate this book to my husband, Jeremiah, and the family that we built together. I would also like to dedicate this book to those who seek the way, the truth, and the life.

TABLE OF CONTENTS

Chapter 1: The Beginning. 1
Chapter 2: The Call. 15
Chapter 3: The First Cut. 33
Chapter 4: The Pandemic. 41
Chapter 5: Isolation 55
Chapter 6: Infected. 81
Chapter 7: I/A. 95
Chapter 8: Disease 117
Chapter 9: Sterility/Pressure 137
Chapter 10: Surgery 153
Chapter 11: Recovered. 173
Chapter 12: Reward. 193

CHAPTER 1:

The Beginning

"In the beginning God created the heavens and the earth" (Genesis 1:1). God created it all: where we came from, where we are, and where we are going. He is with us at all times, through all things. We often forget that He is with us, but He is. Without a doubt, without ceasing, He is with us. Even in the beginning. We all have a beginning, and here is mine.

I have a first memory. Do you? What is it? What is the very first thing you can recall? I remember being in a crib at my grandma Lucy's house, in the room across from the hallway bathroom. Grandma lived in a single-wide trailer that Grandpa had built a den onto. They lived on a farm. The worst farm you ever did see, but I loved it. I loved everything about that piece of land. Perhaps that is why my first memory is there in that crib, singing (at least in my mind I was) a Beatles song. I remember that

I knew everything! I knew my whole life and how it was going to end up, and then God said to me, "You are going to forget it all now." I 100 percent remember responding to God, "All of it?" and God responded, "All of it!" And my memory was wiped! I no longer knew who I was, where I was, where I was going, and what was going to happen.

I was baptized that weekend by my Grandma Lucy by blood and by my Grandpa Manuel by marriage. I found out later that Grandpa Otero, Manuel, loved Lucy from the moment he saw her. He knew that one day he wanted her for his wife, but she was married…in the meantime, he went off to war, and so did her husband, my grandfather, whom I never remember meeting. When he came back home, he learned the war had been hard on her family. She was married to a man who became an alcoholic when he returned from war, and he left her with six children to take care of. I never knew much about my maternal grandfather except three things. Okay, maybe four. He fought in the war, he had six children, he was an alcoholic, and he died of liver failure. That is all I knew about him. Manuel Otero, though…I knew him as a war hero, and so did the rest of the town. He came back to town as a hero, and that is the way he died as well. He came along and took to Lucy's family as if they were his own. I felt unconditionally loved by him, and like he chose me to love. He never had a biological child of his own. But he lived an abundantly full life filled with the love of the entire town. He was one of those people that just loved everyone. It would take him two hours to get through the grocery store because he had to stop and talk to everyone. But it was such an honor to be in his presence. He loved God so much that he went to church *every day*. Except on Saturday, the day of rest. The priest deserves a day off. He stirred his coffee a hundred times *every day*! We all loved him, and he will never be forgotten.

Lucia, Lucy for short, told me that when she went off to kindergarten, there were three other Lucias in her class, so they all had to pick a version of Lucia, and her version became Lucy. So that is how she went from Lucia to Lucy. She taught me so many lessons in life. She did teach me that if you are not happy in a situation you have the right to leave it. She allowed us to see that if you have to work two jobs to pay the bills, then that is what you do. She was a worker until she was able to retire. She was a cashier at a Yellow Front store. She was also a cook at the school. All I ever saw her do was serve her husband. She took care of the farm life and animals, and she also cooked all day long.

She told me of a day when she had all six of her kids; she was a single mother, and she said she was completely out of food and had no idea how she was going to feed her children. She said she did the only thing she knew to do: she got down on her knees and began to pray for some food. She said no sooner had she finished her prayer when a knock at the door occurred, and there was a sack of potatoes, a big, full sack of potatoes. She was able to feed her children, and she said she never struggled to feed them from that day on.

My grandma mentioned to me another story where she was driving in a car with her kids. This was at a time when there were no seat belt laws, and the kids would just run all around the car. She said she was driving down the highway, and a man's voice told her to "Get over now!" loud and firm! So, she moved over and just avoided being crushed by a truck! She said the crazy thing about the story was no man was in the car with her. She said there was no doubt in her mind that God spoke to her right then! He told her to "Get over now." She was convinced that had God not told her to "Get over now," she and all her children would have died that day.

Lucy also survived a scare with cancer. She said to me that when she was younger, maybe in her forties, doctors told her that she had leukemia. She told me, though, that she prayed it away! She mentioned praying away things multiple times to me. She would say, "I do not accept this in Jesus' name, Amen," and she would be healed. Well, unfortunately, that was not the case with her diabetes, although she tries to act like she prayed it away by ignoring the fact that she has diabetes. She never took insulin for it. She lost her eyesight to macular degeneration, but she sure is still alive at the age of ninety-two! My paternal grandmother lived to be in her early nineties as well. This is my story about my walk with God. Unfortunately, I did not get taken closer to God by my paternal grandmother, and my paternal grandfather died when I was young.

Lucy was so key to my faith walk; she made sure that I was in the church if I was in town. I even was able to volunteer as an altar girl a few times, bring out the offering, and shake the bells in the church. Christmas was always special in Las Vegas, New Mexico; we even got snowed in one year. The blizzard of '82, I believe it was. Church on Christmas Eve was held at the church across from Grandma's house, two doors to the right of my little house. Manuel took so much pride in that church!

There was another important lady to my faith walk, my great-grandma Agripina Sanchez. Grandma Pina went by the name Pina. The whole town called her Grandma Pina. She worked as a teacher aide at one of the schools in town. She was a faithful caretaker of children. They flocked to her. She taught me several things while I was in her care. I lived across the street from her when I was four and five years old and while in kindergarten. We met at her house every day after school, where she would take care of me while my mom finished up at work. That was the most special time for me. Occasionally, she would not be home, and I would hang out with her cousin…I think. All I remember about her cousin was that she was always home, lived right next door, and fed me windmill cookies or gingerbread snaps whenever I would have to stay with her. I much preferred to hang out with my Grandma Pina. She taught me how to pray, make coffee, and sew a quilt. She was the best sleeper…me, not so much. I loved to sleep over at her house. We would put on her pj's…which were long nightgowns, just like you see in the movies from the 1920s. We always prayed at the end of the bed on our knees; then we would get in bed, back-to-back, foot-to-foot, and off to sleep. In the morning, she would always complain that I slept like a maniac and kicked her in her one kidney all night long! The only foods I remember her eating were oatmeal, eggs, potatoes, bacon, pinto beans, green chili, and tortillas. She was born in 1910 and lived to be ninety-seven! She would always say to me, "The most important thing is to drink plenty of water!" She would always say that. But she always had hot coffee going, too! She made sure that, at four and five years old, I understood the importance of a relationship with God. I wonder if the other grandchildren had the same experiences with her. I have never thought to ask. Where was my sister all this time? She was never with me. I do not remember her at any of these events.

Speaking of faith walk, my sister played a huge role as well. I will never forget the time we were on a road trip. One of the famous quarterly trips to Las Vegas, New Mexico. I was maybe seven, and we were regular Catholic Church members. I was about to go through my First Holy Communion. I asked my sister, "What happens when you die?" She was eleven at the time, and she said, "When you die, that is it! You are just dead! You cease to exist!" I was like, "What in the world? No way! Hello, what about God?" She told me basically, right then and there, that there is *no God*! Well, since she treated me like she was Satan, I believe that she believed with her whole heart that there was, in fact, *no God*!

As I was reading the Bible for my morning study, I noticed something about the first offering that was offered by Noah. After the land had dried up and Noah had built an altar to the Lord, he took some of all the clean animals and birds and sacrificed burnt offerings on it (Genesis 8:20). I thought about animal sacrifice and what it represents. Each and every meal we eat that has meat in it comes from a living being. God provides these creatures for us to eat and expects that we will accept His gift of life. As we kill a life, we release its spirit back up to the creator, and its flesh provides life for us. It actually becomes a living part of us. I know, I know, it seems kind of weird to think, but everything we eat breaks down into a molecule, and something that our bodies need to survive.

Now, I noticed in Genesis 8:21 that "the Lord smelled the pleasing aroma." I thought about Jesus and how He seemed to love and enjoy fellowship time around a meal. There is no doubt in my mind that God loves food; He loves the way it smells when it cooks. He enjoys it when we gather and cook and fellowship with one another.

Stop and think about mealtime. Is it something we cherish anymore? We have made cooking a chore that we hate. Nobody wants to sit and gather, and everyone has schedules that keep us apart. That is no doubt the workings of the prince of the world. The devil will stop at nothing to distract us and keep us apart. We do not even like food anymore. Most people eat food that is all flavor and no nutrients. This is not food that is produced by God. God made food perfect, and we alter it and make it imperfect by breaking it down and adding chemicals to it so it will last longer because we do not trust God to provide our daily bread. Now, it seems everyone is allergic to all the food we eat. Makes absolutely no sense to me. It just tells me that we are starting to see the effects of what altering our means of food will do to us.

God promised in Genesis 8:21 to never curse the ground again because of humans…so specific. So, there is not anything that we humans can do to cause God to curse the ground. God said that "every inclination of the human heart is evil from childhood" (Genesis 8:21). These are the words from God! The human heart is evil from childhood… there it is! Straight from the mouth of God. We are born with a human heart that is evil! We must be brought into the family of God. We must be chosen by God into His family. Do you remember your first encounter with God? I do… So, was I chosen before I was born? Of course! *So were you*! But we are still born human. Therefore, God will come knocking on our hearts throughout our lives, and eventually, He will move in and kick out the evil that you're born with, and He will envelop your heart and fill it with love, peace, joy, and happiness all the days of your life.

My sister, in her immaturity, was so key to me needing to seek out more about God and find out if He exists or not. My quest for more information started right then and there. I have my sister to thank for the reason why I doubted the presence and existence of God. She had such a negative mindset and attitude about family, love, and God that I felt like she was against everything that God stood for. Not that she was doing evil things or even being a bad person. She just had a negative mindset about all things. She accepted the lifestyle my dad had and loved fantasy and science fiction. I never liked any of that stuff. No matter what happened to us as children, I have to thank her for who I am. She was always bigger, stronger, smarter, faster, taller, and wiser than me. She was able to do everything first. I got hand-me-downs of everything, and she got new everything. She had all of Dad's love; I had all of Mom's. It just is what it is. Because of her, I was left alone in an apartment to fend for myself at the age of eighteen years old. She abandoned me in Colorado, and from that time on, I had to figure life out. That is when my boyfriend at the time, Jeremiah, and I started to cling even tighter together, but it took a bit before we would live together.

At the age of seven, I had a revelation, and from this day forward, I stuck to this opinion. It was the morning after a suicide was discovered along my morning path to school. I knew what had happened in the woods off the marked path. I was alone and scared. I knew someone had died in the woods, and I felt afraid of his ghost. I felt that there was a presence with me, an imaginary friend. So, I talked to my imaginary friend, and I realized at this very moment that my imaginary friend was Jesus! He told me that I did not need to be afraid and that He was always with me. He told me that He would never leave me again and that I was safe with Him. That I could go through the path, and I would be fine. I mustered up my courage and walked through the path, and He was right! I was fine. From that day forward, I began a very close, special friendship with Jesus, my savior. That is all He would be to me for the next thirty-seven years: my Savior.

This is not necessarily a story about how I got saved, though. Everyone writes about how they got saved. I am going to write a story about how my Savior became my Lord, too.

CHAPTER 2:

The Call

I was sitting outside in my pickup truck, a 2018 Dodge Ram Bighorn 4x4 with a custom grill and manufactured lift. She was a beauty! It was break time at one of my three jobs, on a beautiful warm day, October 2, 2018, when my phone rang. You know when it rings, and you are holding it, so you are startled? I did not recognize the number, but nobody ever calls me, so I answered.

"Hello."

"Hi! This is so-and-so; I am calling from The Spine Clinic to confirm your appointment tomorrow at 9:30 a.m. with Dr. C.F. (Neurologist)."

I was completely confused because I knew for a fact I had not called any clinic and set up any appointments. For reference, during this time, I had three jobs, and I was going to school to finish my bachelor's degree in nursing. I did need to see a doctor, but I did not make this appointment. Wait, where is she calling from again? What time?

"I am sorry, ma'am; where did you say you were calling from again?"

"Dr. C.F.'s office, The Spine Clinic."

"Yes, ma'am, give me one second to get a paper and pen."

"Of course, just let me know when you're ready."

Being that I am a nurse and on a break at work, I most definitely had a pen and paper in my pocket on hand, and I was ready within seconds to jot down the information she read off, to begin with. I knew that the day was tomorrow for the appointment, and I also knew I was available because it was a Wednesday, and I am always off on Wednesdays to work on homework that is due on Thursday; I just needed more information.

"Okay, ma'am, I am ready; go ahead with the time again."

"Okay, tomorrow at 9:30 a.m. with Dr. C.F. Did you need the address?"

"Yes, please." I proceeded to write down the information for the appointment, and then I was a little weirded out that a neurology center called me. I was having tons of issues with my neck, and I was getting headaches and having issues with grip strength and feeling in my right hand. I was currently seeing a neurologist who was giving me Botox injections in the crown of my head to help with the headaches I was having. I have had neck issues since I was fourteen years old. It was finally time for me to get my neck imaged and see if there were any actual issues. I kept that appointment and started my journey with Dr. C.F. He has given me pain injections to help diagnose and treat the cause of spinal/nerve pain. Here is the thing that I was so unaware of at the time: I did not make that appointment with Dr. C.F. Who did? I was too busy at the time to even stop and be amazed. I was like…hmm, *God*? Okay, I will obey, but I was unaware that that was the call that would start something that I could not stop. Something that I could not control. Something that would take me from wanting to die to almost dying, to almost dying again, to slowly dying…if I choose to just give in to pain. If you accept *pain*, you accept *death.* Well, I am going to take you through what that phone call started; it is something that I am continuing to fight daily right now as I write these words to you. I am being obedient because *I do not want* to be this way forever! I need to write this to you before the miracle happens because I 100 percent believe that *I am going to be healed* and *live an abundant life* right *here on earth*, because it is what *God* has promised me! However, obedience always comes before blessings.

The exam was uneventful, and he sent me for imaging. The imaging revealed a lot of damage. From C3 to C7, there were changes in my neck. He told me that he would have to refer me directly to see the neurosurgeon, Dr. J.G. He also told me that I was not to lift another thing over five pounds, and to this day, I have not been cleared to lift over five pounds. Obviously, I did not listen to him right then and there. I was in a fitness program, where just a few days before, I was farmer-carrying forty-pound weights around the building in each hand and squatting 140 pounds. Five pounds? This doctor was out of his mind; that was not going to happen. But something in the back of my mind was telling me that I should probably listen. I was having severe headaches and having issues with eating. Something was off, but nobody could find anything. I had seen many doctors trying to find the issue I was having with getting lightheaded, dizzy, and fainting after my morning breakfast. My whole world was about to be flipped upside down. The problem was I did not realize how much my life was going to make a 180-degree turn right away. It was going to take more than a year from that moment to really open my eyes.

Jeremiah and I were simultaneously starting a new business venture, and I was having my life turned completely upside down all at the same time. I was working three jobs during this time and pursuing an opportunity to be coached and mentored by a couple who had taken complete control over time and money and were financially independent. That opportunity alone is the reason I even took the time to look honestly at what my priorities and values were. At this point in my life, working three jobs and still pursuing education, I needed to know what they knew! If they were not breaking man's laws or God's laws, I just needed to know. On October 10, 2018, Jeremiah and I were sponsored into business ownership by the most incredible people. We did not realize it then, but we were falling in love with our sponsors and mentors. We always enjoyed a good adventure, so off we went to start an adventure of a lifetime, one that would teach us far more than we ever hoped to learn. Earth angels are people who carry the Holy Spirit, and they will ignite a love for Christ that, deep down, already exists. Sometimes, God will place you in just the right place, at just the right time, to meet an earth angel in God's *time*.

Timing is everything, and God has the perfect timing. The only thing wrong with our timing is that it is not God's timing. Each person is on their own adventure. I do not believe my adventure is any more significant than anyone else's. In fact, I genuinely believe that if you look back on your life, you will see that you have felt the same as me throughout your journey from time to time.

As I write my past few years down for you, it is not to make you feel like you haven't gone through enough. That you are weak. That you are not chosen. That you are not special. That you are not extraordinary. I am writing this with a hope and a prayer that you will find that you have just as much strength in you as I do in me. That we all carry the exact same strength within us, and His name is Jesus Christ. If you have not ever been introduced to Jesus Christ, please allow me right now to introduce you to Him. *Do not stop reading this book*! He is just my friend, remember? Would you not want to meet my husband if I introduced you to my husband? I am a member of the church body. No, that is not a physical church, but *the church* that my friend Jesus Christ came to start. I used to be rude, controlling, and skeptical, then I met Jesus Christ, and now I am caring, submitted, and faithful.

This is the story of how I went from being a sinner, saved by grace, to a saint, submitted to my Lord Jesus Christ. This is the part some of us struggle with, and I am guilty of being a sinner who had accepted that no matter what, I was saved. The truth is I was saved, and so are you, in my opinion. We all are; that is the entire reason why God humbled Himself, came down to earth, was born of a virgin, died for our sins, rose back to life three days later, and then ascended to the Father, where

He sits on the right-hand side of our Father, but not before sending the Holy Spirit to live and dwell within all of His followers. This is where things get a little tricky for us Christians on earth. We accept our Savior, and then the enemy comes to attack. Before we have a chance to repent and change our mindset, the enemy gets his army ready to attack. And he is good at attacking our weaknesses or the things we have no self-control over. Go ahead and think about it. What are your weaknesses or things you allow to control you? Do not worry; you will hear all about mine soon enough.

In December of 2018, we had just kicked off our business and had started learning the fundamentals of what it takes to own a business. We had other believers to guide us along the way. One of the key things they taught us was to start living through our values. I realized right then and there that we were not living in alignment with our values. So, we started to align our life with our values. They helped us put ourselves on a professional, personal budget, and we started to take control of our finances. We had a lot of leaks and cracks that needed to be fixed up. In fact, we had leaks and cracks in our marriage.

There are times in life when we can get so busy that we do not notice when we have leaks. I was working as a *per diem* nurse at three places, and I was making a ton of money, but I was suffering in pain and needed to figure out why my arm was not working properly. At the same time, we started to get focused on our finances, values, marriage, and family; it seemed I started to get attacked by the enemy physically. Is my physical body a weakness? Why would the enemy attack my body? At this point, I was in straight-up survival mode, and I did not have the maturity to stop and look at what was happening. I only had time to react.

    I had been referred to a chiropractor by the neurosurgeon. He reviewed my X-rays and adjusted my back and neck on that visit. Two days later, I was in so much pain I could hardly walk, and I was having trouble holding in my urine due to the severe pain in my lower back. I followed up with the chiropractor a few days later because he was closed for the weekend. He was worried about the situation and referred me to the ER. I already had a surgical consult scheduled with Dr. J.G. for my neck a few days later, so I followed up with him, and we proceeded with my neck surgery, knowing I would be resting my back and could also pursue treatment at the same time as repairing and recovering my neck. I went into the chiropractor's office crying in pain. He felt terrible, and I knew, as a nurse, how he must feel. I could understand that, as a medical professional, sometimes we do hurt to heal. Isn't that what surgery is? We cut into you to repair a problem within you. An injury has to occur in order to repair an injury or problem within.

I recently read in the Bible about the first surgical procedure that happened. It was performed by God on Adam (hypothetically). Genesis 2:21 says, "So the LORD God caused the man to fall into a deep sleep; and while he was sleeping, he took one of man's ribs and then closed up the place with flesh." Why? "No suitable helper was found" (Genesis 2:20). God cut Adam, the very first man, because there was no helper that was suitable for him on the earth. He had only, at this time, made animals, but God knew that man would need a suitable helper to meet his needs. Someone who could not be found without being cut first. The reason he had to be cut was because he had to find what was within him. God took from within Adam his own flesh and bone and created a woman. There was nothing suitable to fulfill his purpose outside of him. Do you ever feel, as you travel through the journey of life, that you have been cut and bled along the way? Maybe God is trying to cut something out of you that is deep within.

I could go all the way back to the first time I cut myself as a child. I absolutely remember the first three times I was cut and bled badly enough to get attention or stitches. I remember reaching into the fridge for a jelly jar in the middle of the night, and it fell on my toe and cut me. I was maybe two or three. We lived in Houston, Texas, for all of these injuries. I cut my left pointer finger on a can in the trash can…I was two or three, reached into a garbage can and into a can, and cut my finger. I remember my dad ripping off his shirt and wrapping it around my finger and it being bandaged for a while after. I also was riding my bike at three or four years old, in the backyard with my dog, "Candy;" my dress got caught in the bike wheel, and I flipped over the front of my bike and cut open my chin. I got stitches for that one, too. I wonder what happened to that dog? Those were the injuries I remember. I had some type of rash all over my body and was in the hospital for a minute at two or three. I remember getting in trouble *all* the time because I would not eat when they wanted me to. So they would send me to bed hungry. That is why I got out of bed and got into the trash and fridge. My family struggled with me as a child. I would tell my mom and dad that my stomach hurt, but they never did anything about it. I would get into huge fights at the dinner table with my parents growing up. Eventually, I started to win the arguments, and also my parents started to go out to the bar four to five nights a week, so dinner as a family slowed down. I was able to control what I ate, and this is where my control issues became focused. When I became a teenager, I started cutting my skin. Eating caused internal discomfort that was ignored as a child by the people I love, and cutting was ignored by everyone around me. I did not feel loved as a teenager at all. I started looking for love in anyone who I could get to pay attention to me. Which became my "friends."

I became a vet tech in 1999, and from that day until I walked away from that profession, I had a healing wound at all times! *At all times*! Even during the times I was healthy, I would work out so hard at the gym that I would feel constant pain. Is it that I only feel like I am alive if I feel pain? It is not love I feel when I am in pain. God cut Adam because He loved him, right? He had to be cut or hurt physically in order for God to complete him. We are cut because that is what must be done to fulfill our purpose. There is something within us that will complete the process. Now, does that mean that if we have never undergone surgery or had a serious injury in life, we will never be complete? Or that we are not chosen? Absolutely not! Pain is pain! Not all pain is physical, but all pain makes us stop and consider the breath that moves in and out! The only thing that keeps our heart beating is the breath that flows in and out of our lungs.

Have you ever had the "wind knocked out of you" or pain that hurt so bad you could not inhale or exhale? Both are vital for living. If you got up right now and, as fast as you could, sprinted around your block, do you think it would hurt to breathe in? Think about the air flowing in and out. *It hurts!* Sometimes, it hurts so bad that you cannot breathe!

That is why if you have ever had surgery or been in the ER, the nurses and doctors repeat over and over, "Take a deep breath," because when we stop breathing, we stop our hearts from beating. You never think about breathing until the pain hurts so bad you can't inhale or exhale. Think about a time when you had pain so bad that it hurt to breathe in and out. It may not be physical pain; it may be spiritual or emotional. This is the pain that I had in my lower back when the chiropractor ruptured my L5-S1, and that pain persisted with every step I took from that day on. It felt like I was being stabbed in my lower spine. The MRI report revealed a ruptured L5-S1. I would start PT in February 2019 for post-op ACDF C4-C6 and surgical prevention for my L5-S1.

My neck was cut but healed quickly; my back, though? That was another story. This started the downfall of my not being able to work out. I hurt at work, but I had no choice but to push through. We were getting our finances together, and I was never cleared to full duty and was unable to return to two of my jobs. I was down to one job, and that was extremely part-time. I was gaining back all the weight I had lost and losing all of my self-esteem at the same time. Because I was sharing my story with everyone I could and trying to build a solid business foundation and customer base, I was losing friends fast. The association I was working with was so instrumental during this time. There is nothing like having brothers and sisters who are in the same storm as you in life. We are all in different boats but riding in the same storm.

For whatever reason, I was stuck in what felt to me like a hopeless situation. My back was getting worse with each step, and like I said, I was gaining back all the weight I had lost. I could not work as much outside of the house, so I felt like I needed to finally buckle down and help build our business foundation. I had no idea at the time that I would be breaking down physically, but start to build myself up spiritually and mentally. The thing is, we cannot build anything up until we break down what was. We must fully die to ourselves before we can rebuild.

I did not completely surrender my life just yet, but when someone unintentionally placed their hands on me to help me, when we came together, the energy that flowed from him to me was not positive; it was negative. That is what took me to a place that would make nothing on this earth, nothing able to soothe the pain that I would feel the moment my eyes would open. The type of pain that makes you want to stop breathing, stop living, stop being, and die, to actually die and be with God. But I had to ask if He made the appointment to start with, was this the path He was leading me down? Even though the unbearable pain started with the ruptured disc, the process had started, well, the day I was born, but I was planted the day the phone call was made. The seed was fertilized the day my back ruptured, but the root had not started to take hold yet, *oh, no*…God has a way of gardening that I have started to learn over the years. I would have been more observant, but at this time in my life, during the planting, I was too busy to recognize that God had even planted me. I believe it is important to mention that my biological father had just passed away a few months earlier.

I think it is safe to say that God made the appointment for me to see Dr. C.F. (neurologist), who sent me to see Dr. J.G. (neurosurgeon), who sent me to see Dr. Back Snapper (chiropractor), who sent me into a deep, dark depression. I was so busy I didn't even recognize what was occurring to me, in me, or through me. I answered the call and showed up to the appointment, and from there, I have been doing that over and over and over and over and over and over again, from one appointment and meeting scheduled to another. When I was working three jobs and going to school, people would ask me how I kept it straight. I would tell them I showed up wherever my calendar told me to that day. I never missed a meeting or appointment. I supposed that could be why God chose me. I was not allowing Jesus to be my Lord, but I did accept Him as my Savior. When I got the call, I knew He was coming to rescue me, so I showed up to the appointments that I had scheduled in my calendar. The next appointment would be the first cut.

CHAPTER 3:

The First Cut

Do you remember the very first time you were cut? I cannot say that I do, for sure. My memory of this story is not my own; it belongs to my mother, I guess. I may not have the memory, but I do have the scar. One of the first cuts that I received was from a food can. I reached into the trash can at the age of two and sliced my left hand's pointer finger (phalange number two) wide open. My dad ripped off his white T-shirt (which I always remember him wearing), wrapped it around my gushing finger, and held it all the way to the hospital, where I received a few stitches and a massive bandage (there once was a photo, I remember). Going into the trash can after a food can? I was looking for food. Maybe? I do remember being oddly obsessed with pinto and green beans at this age, so maybe I just wanted one green bean from the can.

I am still very food-motivated, but who isn't? I

do not remember the injury at all, but I do still have the scar, and that was just the first of many stitches that I would receive in the future. Some people go their whole entire lives without ever having surgery or stitches. Others start out getting stitches on the day they are born, and some babies even have surgery before they are born. God chooses when we receive the first cut in life. The one thing I know now that I did not know then is that even though we do not recognize it at the time, God is with us from the first breath to the first cut. When we bleed, God bleeds, too.

My neck surgery was scheduled for January 19, 2019, and many preoperative visits would also need to occur. I started entering them into the calendar and showing up, just like I do. One of those appointments was the first spinal surgery I would have. I remember being concerned with really only one thing; okay, two things. Number one, would I be able to get back into the gym in a few weeks? Two, what would people think of my scar? I took a picture of my neck the day before surgery. We had a meeting the evening before surgery from eight p.m. to midnight, so I put on a suit, looked at myself, and made a conscious note that I would never see my neck again without it looking like someone had tried to kill me. My throat would look like someone had tried to slice my head off forever. I was more concerned about my appearance than how my neck would "feel" post-operatively. I did not feel like the surgery would be a big deal. I worked with Dr. J.G's patients post-operatively at the hospital, and they always did great post-operatively, so I felt totally comfortable with the surgical procedure. I was just worried about how people would judge me. Would they think I tried to kill myself? Someone tried to kill me? Would they think I am crazy? Would they feel sorry for me, that I had a serious injury? I always wondered how someone received their scars; there is always a "story."

I knew that the symptoms that I was feeling were actually far worse than what I was willing to admit to myself. The thing is, as a nurse, I would be concerned if anyone had the symptoms I was having with loss of sensation and strength. I just was so used to adapting and overcoming in life that I didn't even recognize when I was reverting to fight mode, and my body was about to get stuck in "fight mode." When our bodies suspect danger, we automatically choose "fight or flight"? I have always been a "fighter," always. I have never ever run away from a challenge, and I was not about to start now. I signed my consent form, kissed my husband goodnight, and woke up on the other side of surgery.

My recovery was about to begin, but first, my body was already starting to respond to the ruptured L5-S1. My left hip was hurting, and an MRI was scheduled, as well as a picture of my lower back. My follow-up, post-operatively, was with the PA; she started physical therapy for my L5-S1, and she said it was "ruptured." She said that surgery was the last option and that I should start therapy for my neck post-operatively and lower back immediately. I did manage to get them to clear me for the last trip I would take for a while, and that was a trip to Europe; a month after neck surgery, I did travel to Europe. It was an amazing experience, but not what this is about. What I do want to note is that, at the time, I did know that this would be the last trip I would go into debt for. I am planted. When your roots are deep, you can't travel. Sacrifices were starting to happen. Slowly, things would start to be taken. I just did not realize how long they would be taken for at the time.

Christmas 2018 was the last time I was on a snowboard. I am here to tell you that it *was* the last time that I was on a snowboard, but not *the last* time I will be on a snowboard. I *will* snowboard again. I am working toward recovery. The cutting was just beginning for me, though…one cut leading to the next and the next.

This seems to be how my life has always been. I went from one cut to the next growing up. I loved animals, and I chased them my whole life, and they cut you when you catch them. I spent seventeen years being cut by animals and receiving a paycheck to do so. I started working as a vet tech in 1999, and I had that job until 2016. I had an open wound every single day for seventeen years. There has rarely ever been a time in my life where I was not being wounded physically or emotionally, just like I am sure a lot of you are.

I am not sitting here thinking that I am so unusual that I am the only person who has been through a hard life. I actually felt a lot of the time like I had such a great life that I did not have anything to complain about. My parents got divorced as a kid, but so did most kids' parents. I was not rare or unusual, so I did not think anything of it. My parents would go out and party four to five nights a week from the time I was eight until I was sixteen; that was my age when my mom left me. My mom left my dad when I was four. My mom left my stepdad when I was sixteen. My sister and stepdad left me when I was eighteen. There it is; I have been on my own since I was eighteen years old.

That is the age I was when my mom gave me $4,000 cash and basically said I was on my own. At the time Jeremiah broke up with me, I had a pocket full of money and a car. I went on a road trip only to return homeless. The lesson I learned from that experience inspired a poem that was chosen from a newspaper contest to be published and inspired me to start keeping and writing in a journal. I learned that yesterday is always past, tomorrow never comes, and today is all we have. I learned that I had one day to deal with, and that was the current one. I needed to learn how to get through one day at a time and that the only person I could ever depend on was me. Each and every day, the only person I could ever depend on was me. I also believed God was with me. I felt His presence, and I have always felt His presence. I have always just been too focused on me to actually be able to hear, see, feel, smell, and taste Him. Is any of that possible?

Feeling is physical, mental, and emotional. When Dr. J.G. was cutting into my neck on January 19, 2019, he was cutting into me because I was having problems with my physical feelings. I could not feel the tips of my fingers anymore. I could not, not feel the pain gnawing on my C6, the pinched nerve I have had since I was fourteen years old. I was in gymnastics at the time, and that was when the coach missed his spot, and I landed right on my head, flipping backward. That was when my injury happened initially to my neck. I was in that gym at Lakewood High School when I hurt my neck, and I was in that gym when I saw Jeremiah again before the school year, a few years later.

At sixteen years old, I was a freshly confirmed

Catholic, but I started to attend a Baptist Church with Jeremiah and his family. I started to become curious about religion, and I started to learn about different religions and philosophies and experimenting with drugs. Jeremiah got me involved in all kinds of things at sixteen; church was one of them, but so were drugs. He was very religious and very bad. That was the start of confusion in me because Jeremiah could be so good and so bad all at once. I was about to go to school to learn how to be "religious" from his family. This is where I was stuck for years in my mentality. This is not a great place to be. I argued about "religion" with Jeremiah constantly and was getting more and more lost. Without a family to guide me, all I had was Jeremiah and his influence on me. I was not strong enough at the time, and I let the world win. I accepted Christ as my savior. I called on Him whenever I needed Him, which would be often, too often. This was the start of being lost.

CHAPTER 4:

The Pandemic

Things were looking up. I was healing from back surgery, and my neck was pretty pain-free by this point. I even went back to work. I had maybe been back for a week when, all of a sudden, the world shut down. At the same time a virus was taking over the world, something I lovingly refer to as "Shamus" was taking over my life. I was still dragging around a very painful, cramping, gnawing, nagging, pins-and-needles feeling leg. I was recovering slowly from the back surgery, and then I started to experience super bad heartburn. Whenever I would eat, I would have indigestion and heartburn, which I had never suffered from except when I was pregnant with my children. I decided that I would give up dairy and sugar for Lent. Even though I am not a practicing Catholic, that is one practice that I felt the churches I attended lacked. They did not fast in any way. Lent was the practice of giving up something for forty days in remembrance of what Christ did for you on the cross. At the time, that was my complete understanding of Lent.

I have always had an intolerance to dairy and had gained forty-plus pounds since my back rupture, so I figured I would help two issues at once. On Ash Wednesday, I went to a Catholic mass actually, and I had ashes put on my forehead, and the words uttered to me, "Remember, you are dust, and to dust you shall return." My journal reports that I lost 9.25 inches and twelve pounds in weight. Unfortunately, the fast did nothing but discipline my mouth from food entering. Most years of my life, I continued to practice Lent, starting on Ash Wednesday. This was the first year I had ashes put on my head since I was a teenager. It felt as though it had ushered me into the next phase of life. Even though during this time, my heart was being called to the Spirit, it was also saying goodbye to a life that was held to a chain called "religion." I did not know it, but that is what was holding me back all along.

At this time, the virus was new and unknown. I honestly think that Coby and I had it in the fall of 2019. I had to take him to the pediatrician (I think his last one), and she said that the "flu" was starting early this year and that it was a very aggressive strain. Poor woman had no idea she was dealing with COVID at the time. Since we had already had a less severe strain, when the deadly one came around, we were not affected by it. A lot of people were testing positive. Coby had symptoms in the spring of 2020, and for three weeks, he tested positive. We all just lived in the same house, with no major quarantine after ten days. We had all been exposed to him during his contagious time, so we all just hunkered down in the house for a few weeks. The health district called us and let us know that after ten days, we were all free to move about the world. So we went about our lives, mask on, hand sanitizer in pocket. I was happy to see everyone so aware of germs. I have always hated germs, so the new "clean-conscious" world was not too hard for me to adjust to. As a nurse, the mask was easy to adjust to as well.

This is not a book about a virus, but not addressing how I was feeling at the time would be leaving out a huge reason why I initially had the time to start studying Jesus and His character. I opted during the pandemic to forgo my shifts at the Surgery Center because I knew that there were other families that needed the income more than we did. I wanted other families to have the income, and I was already out of work for three months. Since we were focusing on taking control over time and money, we had our finances on the right track. During the spring and all the way through the summer, I was basically out of work.

I graduated in the spring of 2020. I was one of the graduates of 2020 who did not get a graduation ceremony because of the pandemic. I have never walked in a cap and gown. I was finally going to graduate. I did not graduate high school; I got a GED. When I graduated from Bel-Rea Institute of Veterinary Medicine with an Associate's Degree of Applied Science in Veterinary Medicine, we had a graduation ceremony, but there was no gown. When I graduated from the College of Southern Nevada with an Associate's Degree in Applied Science in Nursing, we had a pinning ceremony that I loved. Then, I chose to wait to walk in a cap and gown until I finished my Bachelor's Degree from Nevada State. I graduated in spring of 2020 with a Bachelor's Degree in Nursing. So that was one thing I felt like I was always striving for and never reaching.

I thought I had closed a chapter in life. I was not going to pursue education any longer. I had finally found what I had been looking for my entire life. I found a purpose. The business had finally given me a purpose. At least, that is what I thought at the time. I started to focus all of my energy on educating myself on this business, and I just saw Jesus as the ultimate mentor. I started to pursue a relationship with Jesus; I wanted to understand His character, how He responds to situations, and how He treats others. Just like everyone else, as I was locked in, I was being confronted with the person I had been avoiding for forty years: me. Just like the Israelites, they were lost for forty years, and so was I. Our mentor mentioned in a meeting that he felt like God had put everyone in a "time-out!" It absolutely felt that way. I was not only in time-out from work, but I had started to have even worse issues with pain, nausea, discomfort, and bloating whenever I ate a meal. I had friends and family start to notice that I was dropping weight rapidly and not able to eat. I enjoy food, so this was a concern to everyone around me who knew me. I had nurse friends try to push me to see a doctor, and I did. I saw him for seven months, and after many, many, many tests and procedures, they cleared me of any GI issues. But not before I thought I was going to die! I went in for a routine procedure one day and ended up in the ER the next day. I spent a few days hospitalized and actually wondering if I was dying. I felt like, at this moment, I had a choice, but it was my choice; I could either choose to live or choose to die.

By this time, it is important to note that I am studying God's word daily and feel the Spirit, but I do not understand what this feeling is. I just know that I need to take the Word of God in each and every day and learn as much as possible. I do feel like God chose me, and I chose Him right back. I knew my purpose was to fulfill His will; I had just not submitted to being an open book in front of Him. I had to die to myself first before I could submit to Him. It took for me to get to a point where I was so sick that I actually knew that it was up to me to continue here on Earth.

When I returned to work, I started to work full-time hours. But my back was not okay with this, and I also noticed that my brain and my arm were not talking well. My handwriting was weird, and as I was trying to tie the surgeon's gown, it was as if my hand was struggling to make the connection to my brain. Somewhere, there was a disconnect. I could give you a bunch of medical jargon on what was not working, but to me, it was obvious that in both my physical and spiritual life, there was a disconnect! For forty years, there was something blocking the connection. There was interference. There was not a clear signal from my brain/mind to my hand and from my mind to my spirit. My neurosurgeon consulted with me and decided there was no time to wait. I needed surgery on my neck again. When I found that out, I was devastated. Why? I just had surgery, and my neck finally, for the first time since I was sixteen…*did not hurt*! I can't go through another neck surgery! What choice do I have? Paralysis versus surgery? Is there even an option? You just have to take it! Hand dealt! It does not matter what led me to this point in my life…is there even an option, or do I just have to submit to the situation?

At the same exact time I was doing preoperative procedures for my neck, I was getting my GI looked at thoroughly. Extremely thoroughly. I was getting super lightheaded and dizzy after every meal, and I would get so bloated and feel so much back and stomach pain after each meal. I went in to have some biopsies taken of my GI tract, and because of previous neck surgery, I needed to have my esophagus dilated. Other than a narrow esophagus, no abnormalities were found. But, of course, biopsies were taken to look for microscopic findings. Immediately following the procedure, I started having severe nausea and abdominal pain! It lasted for hours, but I was finally awake enough to be sent home. That started an evening of vomiting that turned into hours of vomiting up blood, and eventually to the ER. One week before neck surgery, I was hospitalized for complications from the biopsy…the bleeding upset my stomach and just started a snowball effect.

I spent a few days in the ER and went five days or more with zero food because I had cleaned myself out for the EGD/colonoscopy, and then two to three days NPO because of a few stomach biopsies.

All biopsies came back great! No issues with my GI, just a random complication. I was discharged home, and I was defeated! I could not eat anything without forcing it in. My stomach hurt so bad, and I could not even get a bite of food in me. I knew, though, that if I did not eat, I would die; you have to eat to live. I had gone six days with no food, and I had to force myself to eat. Despite the pain I felt with each bite, I had to eat to live. I had a moment after I had realized that I was stuck. I had no choice but to submit. Submit to this situation with my health/body, with my *God*, and where He was leading me, but my mind/soul was the thing that I was not in control over. Our souls can be lost. Or it can be saved. I was saved; that was all, though, and I did not even realize that this was not enough. God was about to give me a lesson on what happens when *He* is the *Lord* of your life.

So, I did what I had to do. I took a bite of food. I was already on a different diet that was supposed to help with the gas that was being produced with each and every single meal that I ate. I later would come to realize that the food I was eating was causing the problems I was having. Right then and there...at that time, though, all I knew was that I needed to eat, and that every bite of food and drink of liquid caused physical pain before my biopsies went from just a feeling of heartburn and nausea to straight pain. I knew I was about to have surgery; the GI doctor gave the okay for neck surgery, and I continued with my preoperative testing. Before I knew it, I was back in the hospital for round two of neck surgery. This time, they would do an ACDF of my C6-C7 and make sure that the C4-C6 site still looked good since I was having numbness and connection problems.

It is all about the "*connection*," which is what has been missing all along. The connection to God the Father! I knew the Son, but I did not know the Father or the Holy Spirit. I was saved, but if I died today, what was going to happen to me? The truth was, I had absolutely no idea at all. It was time for me to meet Jesus Christ and study His character. Who God was. I have always been terrified of God; that is a good thing I have learned. Not in the way I was afraid, though. Fear of God is simply a fear of the knowledge that *He* is the Creator, Provider, our Father, and our disciplinarian; if He provides all things, then He can remove all things. I always knew that. I had no understanding of the Holy Spirit. I have learned along the way that I did not fully understand the Holy Trinity, and I all of a sudden became drawn to the Holy Trinity. The Father, the Son, and the Holy Spirit.

Following my second neck surgery, I just fell on my face in my room and surrendered my life. I knew that from that moment on, I was going to continue to go through trials. The medical condition was not going away overnight, and I did not even know if I would be able to return to work, but I knew that I had no choice but to surrender my life and my future to God. I asked for forgiveness of my sins. I got on my hands and knees and begged Jeremiah to forgive me for the way I had treated him through the years. Jesus opened my eyes to the way I had controlled Jeremiah our entire marriage and did not trust him to lead our family the way a man should. Although I knew we both had made mistakes over the years, I was going to let Jesus remove all the *sins* and *stains* in my life, and for that, I felt born again. Jeremiah did not forgive me, not the first, second, or even the third time I asked him to forgive me.

We started to fight again. We had stopped fighting, to be honest, prior to this time, and we had learned to go our separate ways when we disagreed and go to our own corner. The problem with that was that we never solved any of our issues. With the next fight came all the issues we had never worked out. I kept going back to God with each and every fight and asking what the point was. Would Jeremiah ever forgive me? Would he ever trust me? Would we ever be okay? So now I am dealing with my health falling apart and my marriage falling apart, and all the while, I am starting to instill habits that are in alignment with my values. If I am going to be stuck at home, sick, during a pandemic, then I am going to make good use of my time.

I opened up the Bible, and I started to read. I started in the New Testament. It was like all of a sudden I understood exactly what I was reading. I felt just like one of the disciples…I felt like Jesus was saying to me, "Elle, lay down your stethoscope and follow me." I listened, and I dived into His word. His truth. My whole world started to open up. I started to watch a sermon every day as well as reading my Bible. It was as if the words I read and the words the pastors were saying were being spoken to me directly.

I have learned that even though we may not know one another personally, if you are reading this book and you are at your worst or you are at your best...you are *not alone*. God is with you. *God loves you so much.* He made you in His image and formed you to be a creator just like Him. He is amazing! He appears in three forms: the Father, Son, and Spirit. The Father is not the Son or Spirit, but they are all the same. This was such a difficult concept for me to grasp. One day, sitting at work following a biology lab, I looked up at a bag of fluids, and I realized that my understanding of water explained what I could not understand about the Holy Trinity. How can three things all be made up of the same thing but be totally different? What made them different? What made them the same?

There it was: water. H2O. One thing that is always the same but can be in three forms. Steam, ice, and water. As I started to ponder what makes them behave differently, my whole world opened up. Science started to meet the Bible to me, and this is how I finally understood the Holy Trinity.

It was like a light bulb finally turned on. I had no doubt that the Holy Trinity was so important and that I was missing part of the Trinity; I was missing the Spirit. I felt like God *was* with me. That I *was* chosen. What I wasn't was *submitted*! So that is when I was put in isolation.

CHAPTER 5:

Isolation

I felt the Spirit calling me, but I had a lot of work to do to change my heart. The truth is, I had lost the love in my heart when my stepdad, John, passed away. I always felt like he was the only person in the world who loved me unconditionally. I felt like I was left alone when he died. I had my children, who I knew loved me unconditionally, so I started to pour all my time and energy into being as good as I could be for them. John passed away in 2006, and I started pursuing nursing in 2010. That is right: it took me four years to even decide to go back to school. Once I started, though, I finished! I quit once, but I kept going. The whole reason I decided to go to nursing school was because of the time I spent with John as he was being diagnosed with the two separate cancers inside of him that would eventually take his life on earth.

On the day I graduated, I felt John's presence

so strongly. I know he would have been so proud of me just for finishing what I started. He was not a great leader or teacher. In fact, he was a horrible alcoholic, cheated on my mom, and is the reason why my whole world was turned upside down as a teenager when he and my mother decided to get a divorce. I have a lot of special memories with him. The most important one, though, was when he was struggling in the hospital with all that was going on. I asked him if he wanted to go to the chapel. So, I led him to the chapel, and we prayed, lit a candle, and read Psalm 23 in the Bible that was at the altar. I think I may have even read it out loud to him. We read it together. I remember that. He was able to go home from the hospital and die in his own bed, not before calling me and asking for "forgiveness." Of course, I forgave him, and I know that he is in his resting place at peace.

Once John passed away, I started to build a concrete wall around my heart. I was going to protect my heart. My husband and I, at the time, had learned to stay in our own corners. We were just trying to get from one day to the next and make ends meet. I was home during the day with the kids while he worked, then we high-fived in the garage around three, and then I went to work, and he stayed with the kids at night. That is the exact reason that we became complete and total strangers; not only was a wall being built around my heart, but there was no unconditional love coming from Jeremiah or going to him from me. We only knew how to love conditionally at this point. Meaning we had to always be on our best behavior or suffer the consequences. We kept going to church back then, but I plugged right into school and plugged out of my marriage.

As the pandemic was taking over the world, it took a long time for the world to mold and shape us to follow suit. Eventually, though, the entire world would accept that the virus was being treated as a pandemic, and we would all have to change everything about the way we interacted with each other. This would be the biggest indicator of who was related to *truth* and who was living in *fear*.

There was no way I was going to live in fear, but there was a ton of misinformation out there. One thing I know: *truth never changes*! So, when the CDC and WHO organizations kept changing what the "regulations" were, I personally knew that the *truth* was not a part of what was happening. Nothing happens on this earth without the knowledge of God, *nothing*, and that God protects His children. That is all I needed to understand during 2019. I became a good citizen and started to wear my "mask" just like everyone else. The "mask" has, at this point, become a metaphor for everything. What are you hiding behind your "mask"? At this point, who even knows? As a nurse, I had so many mixed feelings about how we were treating society. We were isolating everyone, sick, healthy…the exception was only for "essential" workers. My family is all essential, and everyone but me kept working.

Slowly but surely, the world started to shift. More and more businesses were closed down. It seemed like, offline, all the businesses that were opened were being streamlined down. This was when I realized that people had been wearing "masks" for a long time. The pandemic brought out the ugly side of all of us. It made each of us sit down and seriously take a look at how we were living, what "was" essential, and what wasn't. A lot of people were having financial issues, obviously, and with the majority of businesses being shut down, unemployment was at an all-time high. The people collecting unemployment were loving sitting at home. The government was taking very good care of those sitting at home then. There was not much at first to worry about as long as you stayed in and did not interact with others, according to the news. "Shut up, stay home, and mind your business" was pretty much the message that I was getting from our government system.

There was a lot of political, racial, and just overall injustice and confusion being posted all over the internet. I was asking "friends" and family if they knew what was going on, because I had chosen to turn off the TV and social media due to the association I was involved with prior to the pandemic. This was just a normal lifestyle for them. I had decided that I would not input too much of the media, but I did go out and interact at appointments, and to me, it did not seem like what was being posted online matched with what I was seeing in my community. The people who were reading the internet and watching TV were scared, and the ones who were not were not scared.

The hard part during this time was that it was time to let some friends go. People who I thought were my friends and family let the time and distance between us separate us. The people who really had my back leaned in during my time of need. I had friends who were paranoid about the virus and couldn't wait for the vaccine to come out and other friends who did not trust the quick process of the vaccine release. So, even in the medical field, it seems that opinions vary. The hardest part during this time was the loss of friendships I thought would never die. I was about to face being placed back under the knife. I was going to be cut again. This time, though, all of my friends would not make it to the other side of the cut.

Once I was released from the hospital, I started to undergo a series of GI testing. It took all the way until March of 2021 to clear my GI tract. They could not find any reason at all for why I was having pain. The pain was getting worse, and there were no answers. Test after test came back good, no issues. I could not understand how I could be feeling so much pain in my back and stomach all the time, and nothing at all was showing. I honestly could not eat, and slowly but surely, I started to feel like an outcast.

My friends and family constantly questioned me about weight loss because it was fast and obvious, but there were still no explanations. Every nurse around me (that was a lot) had their own opinion about what was wrong with me and encouraged me to get a second opinion. I did not know what to do or who to turn to. I started to feel alone and isolated; nobody understood what I was going through. Everything hurts! That is when my faith had to take over. Before my neck surgery, my neck did not hurt at all; after that surgery, it does not ever not hurt. As I write this, I have not fully recovered from that second surgery. I have also not had a decent night's sleep. I told my boss I would be leaving for surgery, but the truth was I would never really return. The woman who left that job never returned. When I came back, I was different. I was different because I died during those few weeks. The week I was in the hospital, unable to eat, followed immediately by a life-changing surgery. I was reminded today that you cannot be resurrected until you die. Well, that was when the person that I thought I was would die, and the person that was new in the Spirit was about to be *born*. My name had already changed, and I had already started to work on becoming a more positive version of myself. I was studying my mentor, Jesus.

I underwent surgery on my neck, returned very quickly to PT, and recovered my neck. I was unable to eat, and that issue seemed to continue to get worse. I continued following up with the GI doctor and received every test possible to clear my GI tract. During this time, I was still isolated because of my illness, but also because of the virus. It had seemed to infect all of the areas in my life. Not my physical body, though. To my knowledge, I have only had the virus once, but during this recovery, it was not physically that I was infected with the virus. Like many other people in the world, my life was infected by the virus in every other way than physical.

The virus had made it so that when I was ill and hospitalized, I was alone and isolated. There was nobody with me who cared about me, nobody to speak up on my behalf. I know that I was not the only person who felt alone and isolated. We all felt like God had taken us and put us in a time-out. I could not help but feel like that is exactly how I felt, but on an exaggerated level, because I could not return to work or do anything I could before surgery. My recovery was lonely, except I was blessed to see my daughter at PT. That and being able to spend time with Coby was the highlight of my days. Starting in August 2020, my lesson in submission would begin. The health issues that I was having were leaking into every area of my life…starting with my body and then taking away my job, my marriage, my parenting, my friendships, my business, my mind, and my soul.

This is when Spirit came in and took over my life. I had surrendered to My Savior Jesus Christ once again. I renewed my vow to be faithful and start growing in my walk with Christ. See, I had always believed and felt saved numerous times. Right now, though, I was not feeling saved; I was feeling like I was being punished. The fact that I was closer to God than ever was what made the isolation and pain even more confusing. Why am I being punished when I am finally doing what I feel like I am supposed to be doing? I am spending time with God, praying, and reading the Bible, watching tons of sermons, and still, I am being punished.

During this time of renewal, I had to be completely *born* again! Jesus opened my eyes! In August 2020, after my second ACDF surgery and weeks of struggling to eat and drink, Jesus opened my eyes. It was as if I had been wearing someone else's prescription and could not see a clear picture. I was in my room on my hands and knees, praying in the sun, and I felt the Holy Spirit ascend upon me! It was almost as if I was set on fire. Like an energy I have never felt within me had come alive! From this day forward, when I read the Bible, I have a clear understanding of what I am reading and find new and exciting discoveries in the text. I have learned how to communicate with God. I felt as if I finally had a connection to God the Father! I always felt as if God was watching me and hearing me, just not sure if anything I asked for would be done or if I had the right to even ask for anything.

I never understood the Father, the Son, and the Spirit before that moment. Because the truth was the Spirit in me, but it was not ignited, like there was potential for fire but no spark…until that moment when God ignited the Spirit within me. The Spirit is God-given, God-breathed, and it was not even at that moment that I understood why and how I all of a sudden understood. I knew one thing for sure…something felt different inside of me. I had come to a place where I was so low and had literally what I felt like was no one person on this earth who could or would help me.

I came to a point where I was so low nobody could comfort me, and everyone was scared to even talk to me. They had no idea what I was going through and no idea what to say to me. Even the nurses that I knew were at a loss for words with how to help me or where to send me for help. I called holistic doctors, and they even refused to see me. What are you supposed to do when you are in excruciating pain and you go to the ER, and they send you away without helping you? No person would or could help me. PT just causes more pain to relieve pain, and so it is almost like I am having to endure pain just so I can feel better. It becomes so confusing when you have completely surrendered your life to *God*, and then you feel like the world is against you.

I was searching for answers about what was happening inside my body, my mind, and my spirit. I was finding more answers in the Bible than anywhere else, and the spiritual leaders that I have been following have been opening up my eyes even more to what I am going through. The more I searched outside of myself for answers, the more God sent me to look inside of myself for answers. Jesus and I were having hours and hours of conversation where I was considering every sin that I had committed against God and His people...I thought that if I looked deep enough, I would find the *sin I was paying for*!

With the pain and suffering I am feeling! What did I do? Where did I go wrong? There is somewhere, right? A loving, caring God would not make a perfectly "good" girl suffer like this. Seriously?! There has to be something, and so I have spent the last year and a half thinking, searching, and wondering about my life and what landed me in this spot. Losing weight, unable to eat without pain, unable to sit, stand, lay down without pain? Is there a moment without pain? Not at this point in my life. Not the summer of 2020...and so far, not the winter of 2022. Do I still deserve this? Will this ever end? What is this teaching me?

God wants me to share with you all that He has taught me in the last year and a half. He started teaching me when I was first baptized and started studying His Word, back when I had that Biology course, when He showed me how water was a direct example of how the Father, Son, and Spirit could all exist as the exact same thing, but in three separate forms. The problem was that I got distracted all those years ago with school, work, kids, a home, and a new career. As soon as I was baptized all those years ago, the enemy came along and put my favorite distraction in front of me: books. I started to learn about science and got close with an old/new group of friends. The thing was, I did not even realize that I was allowing myself to be pulled away from God and Jesus and the education that I was receiving from Him. I just thought with all of my heart that I was meant to go to nursing school, so I went. Then I got lost. Now I am found. I was not found before I became *infected* first.

Maybe you are asking yourself…how can I be infected by the enemy if I am saved and have the

Holy Spirit living in me? Truth is, God is with you, but He can not dwell in an infected home. We may accept Christ as our Savior, but the issue is we do not repent and change. We just accept Jesus as a matter of fact and go on with our lives. We never actually change, and we do not allow Christ to lord over our lives. We do not follow Jesus Christ, our Lord and Savior. We follow Jesus Christ the Savior. I was guilty of not allowing Jesus to lord over my life. I became infected by the enemy.

I had come to a point where I was aware of my need for Jesus. I knew that the only one who could save me was Jesus, and so I surrendered my life. I died to myself and rose again to live for my Lord and Savior, Jesus Christ. I realized that I had been created not by Doris and Robert but by God the Father. The creator of the world and all that lives and dwells on it. That Jesus Christ is God the Father, that He humbled Himself to become a man on His Earth. That God came down to earth, was born to Mary, a virgin, and that Jesus is the Son of Mary (The Son of Man) and God the Father (The Son of God). Jesus came and lived on our Earth for thirty-three years.

He spent thirty years being a man and feeling every earthly desire we feel. God loved us so much that He sent His Son to take our place, to be our sacrificial lamb. Jesus is our teacher, our mentor, our earthly example of how we are supposed to live on this earth. He left the Holy Bible, His love story to us. It is a living, breathing love story. It tells us everything we need to know to live a happy, peaceful, joyful, glorious life. As you read the Bible, you will watch the prophets, disciples, and Jesus go through trials and tribulations and teach us all along the way how to behave in a manner that would please God our Father. The thing is, you have to read the Bible to know if it is real or not. You have to read it for yourself. You can't take my word for it. I tried that. You also can't read the cliff notes. Nope, you actually need to pick it up and read it for yourself. You can question the book your entire life, or you can read it!?

I have no doubt in my mind that the words in the Bible are all true. Truth lives inside me now. I had to come to my own realization that I was created by God the Father. Jesus was born of a virgin, Jesus is God the Son, and Jesus gave up His life for you and me so that when we die, when we take our last breath, and our energy goes somewhere…that somewhere can be heaven.

Okay…it is time to address the big thing. What happens to us when we die? That is the question I asked my sister. What happens to us when we die? She said, "Nothing! We just stop breathing! We cease to exist!" Ask yourself this question: What is going to happen to you when you die?

Like many, probably most, I have pondered that question since I asked my sister at six or seven-ish. Here is what my scientific brain understands. We are all made of energy, and energy can not be destroyed; it can only change forms, so when we die, we change forms. That was a good realization for me when I was in my twenties. So even though I could not understand a God who hung the planet, or evolution, or whatever else school was trying to teach me about life as we know it…I knew one thing for sure. We change forms, period. My understanding of that meant the thought of death could be less scary. So where do we go? If you are waiting for an answer, then you are no different than me! Would God want us to just accept everything that we hear without questioning it? Maybe God wants to show us that not only did He do and say everything that is written in the Bible, but He gives us the answers to each and every life question in the Bible. So, what are you waiting for? Go give it a read. There is an answer to where we go when we die. It sounds amazing and magical, and Jesus is preparing that place for us right now.

I have a fact for you. You will leave this world, and so will I. There are two things we do not get out of, that is, being born and dying. The incredible thing is that we can experience death to ourselves so that we do not have to experience death from life. Jesus was sent by God to take the punishment for our sins. It does not seem fair that someone else should have to suffer and die for us. I believe that most of us feel like we do not deserve to have someone take the punishment for us. Many of us do not realize the pain and suffering that was endured for us by Christ so that we would not have to die and be lost. God wants each and every one of us to come to accept that He is the creator and that He sent His Son to die for us so that we can all have everlasting life, so that none of us will be lost.

The Bible explains how we are to treat each other and how we are to live as Christians. The thing is that until I opened up the Bible, I did not know how to behave as a Christian. There were not many examples in my life for me to turn to. The people that I went to church with just grabbed their values on Sunday for an hour, and so did I. I questioned everything about God, Jesus, and the Holy Spirit. I questioned the validity of the Bible. Of course I did; maybe you do, too, or you did at one point. That is exactly what the enemy wants. If we can live our entire lives distracted from the *truth*, then we will be his children and not God's children. The enemy will spend our entire lives coming at our senses. He uses what we can see, touch, feel, taste, smell, and hear.

The moment the Spirit comes to live within us, we will be tempted by the enemy. Jesus was led by the Spirit away from His disciples and family for forty days, where He was tempted by the devil. Jesus was isolated and tempted. If Jesus, God Himself, was tempted by the devil, then you would have to believe that you, too, could have been tempted by the devil one time, or two million. Jesus is the only man that we know of who lived a sinless life. We should be grateful for that fact. It is that fact that makes it so that we are forgiven for our sins. All we are to do is accept that Jesus was crucified on the cross for our sins. Jesus and God made a covenant that included *you*, *me*, and the Holy Spirit. They made a pact that Jesus would take the sin of the world, that no matter what sin you or I committed or commit, we are completely and wholeheartedly forgiven for any and all of our sins. Jesus has washed us clean with the shedding of His blood on the cross. Once we accept that nothing we can do in this lifetime will ever earn us a spot in heaven or lose us a spot in heaven. We are nothing but sin before we accept Christ and nothing but clean after we accept in our hearts.

The *truth* of *who* we are and *whose* we are, once we surrender our lives…again I said *surrender* our lives to Jesus, once we are *obedient* and choose to follow Christ's example and repent for our *sins*, then God will send the Holy Spirit to live and dwell within us. This gift is available for everyone reading this. You are all forgiven, and you are all chosen. You were all created by God, not your mom and dad, by

God. Your conception was magical; your birthday, time, and place were chosen specifically for *you*. You are a perfect piece to God's big, huge puzzle. You fit perfectly. You have a purpose for God. It is not for me to tell you what the purpose of your life is. It is time for you to take your chosen place in God's kingdom. It is just a decision, a choice to believe. What so many others that have gone before us have chosen to believe.

The thing is, though, you have your own mind, your own heart, and your own soul. You get to choose. God has allowed each and every person free will. The ability to say, "I *will*," the choice to say, "I *am willing*" to lay down "my" life, pick up "my cross," and live for Him. I read in the Bible that Jesus said if you live for me, you will never die, and I believe Him. There is no shortage of information in this world; there are many books that explain the Bible, but why in the world would you allow any other person but you to decide your fate in this world? This is *your* life. You should be the one to decide what you believe.

Jesus was isolated as soon as the Holy Spirit descended upon Him, and so was I. I felt like I was literally dying in my body. I was feeling so much pain, and there was nothing I could do to make it any better, so I started to distract myself with input. I started to read and study the Bible. Listen to one-to-many sermons a day and write my thoughts down. I was trying to understand what was happening in my own body, my mind, and my spirit, and realizing that they all go hand in hand. As soon as the Spirit opened my eyes, I understood that I had a job to do. If there is any way that I can help someone avoid the pain that I am facing, then I must try to help. We are all bridges to Jesus. You were meant to pick this book up and read it because you need to know that you have a place. You belong to God; you are exactly how God needs you to be in order to reach a certain individual and bring them home. We are all connected, just like you see with our cell phones. If you can understand how a floating spacecraft can connect you to your friends 24/7, but do not think God can hear and see all that you do? Do we even live on the same planet?

All I needed to believe that God exists was to watch *live* TV! That seems impossible to me! I understood that as soon as I believed and accepted

Jesus as my Lord and Savior, I was given God's cell phone number. We have a connection now that did not exist before. Before what you may be asking? Before I accepted Jesus as my Lord, I was a Christian who had accepted Jesus as my Savior many, many times. Over and over again. I always knew I was a sinner. I just liked to control my own fate. This was the missing link all along. Through forty years of my life, I had no Spirit. When we think about our lives, we think of them in three parts. We have our mind, body, and spirit. Some say mind, body, and soul. We have a physical body, a thinking mind/soul, and a spirit (good/evil). Our spirit is what I think we tend to worry about, most importantly, where it will go when we die. The part that we all recognize can not be destroyed; it can only change forms. This is the part of us that can become infected with the world/the enemy.

I have to go back to my physical body and how my body became infected. I was saved and gave my life to Christ at age seven. The Holy Spirit was living and dwelling within me. I was a candle that burned, and because I was asking questions, my family was placing me in the environment that I was craving. I needed to understand what happened when we died. I sure as heck was not going to take my sister's word for it. I had heard something that I believed, and I wanted to understand more. My great-grandma, grandma, and mom (all maternal) started to take me to church as a child. I was involved closely until age thirteen...as soon as we moved, all sorts of things changed. I switched schools, and my friend list changed. I moved from Golden, Colorado, where the church was, to Lakewood, Colorado. My parents started to struggle, and the next three years would be confusing.

I started to search for the love that was falling apart at home. I had my first serious boyfriend, and since I had a terrible association and zero parental guidance, I did what everyone else seemed to be doing and had sex with my boyfriend. Once we broke up, I started to cut myself to feel something. There was an emptiness that I had a hard time filling. I was going through the process of being confirmed in the Catholic religion, and I was a sinner. A terrible one. I was confirmed. The shame was not covered. I did not tell the priest what I had done. I did not even agree with that. So, I got into the next relationship, and the next, and the next... and then I met Jeremiah.

He saved me from an enemy. We started going to church with his family. They acted nothing like the Jesus they preached about, but I did feel like I was at home and with the person I was meant to be with. I gave my heart and soul to Jeremiah, and we started our life together. Two saved Christians. I can only talk from my vision at the time, and at this time, I was perfectly fine being saved; I accepted that and called on God when I needed Him. The truth was, though, I was infected with a negative mindset that I could not shake. One that I had allowed to fill me up when I was so empty.

Once you become infected, the cure is greatly affected by what the pathogen is. That determines how the infection is treated. I went from having an abscess to being septic and being close to death. There are many ways to get injured in life. Our physical body can endure and withstand so much that I marvel every time someone is healed from a flesh wound or a miracle cures someone. In fact, I have based my entire life on the marvel of injury and repair. I never in my life imagined that I would undergo an issue that not only I could not solve but that the doctors would not be able to solve. This pushed me to the point of begging that my life would be ended. God answers prayers, you guys! My life did end! I surrendered it to Jesus Christ; I begged Him to be the *Lord* of my life! Then, I was sent to the wilderness to be tempted and to suffer.

I believe it is time to enter my word association into the book. See, when I died to myself and was raised again to live in Jesus, I was fully repented and surrendered. I was born again through baptism on July 4, 2021. It would become this amazing moment in time when I could honestly say I felt the presence of God; I felt that He was pleased with me and that we had an understanding that I was to become a disciple of His Word. As soon as I was baptized, I started to receive "downloads" from God. My first one was about water and bonds, positive and negative energy, and basically a bunch of words and associations I could not understand. I just became excited about what God was choosing to speak to me and started to ask God to use me as a vessel, and that whatever I was learning could be something that I could pass down to future

Christians and leaders in the world. I cannot even express the level to which my prayers have been answered. I have seen miracles transpire and God accomplish greatness in our lives. I have so much to share with everyone, but for now, we are going to focus on the word "infected."

CHAPTER 6:

Infected

How do we get infected? First things first, a foreign body has to enter our body, and then a reaction occurs in our bloodstream. I go back to the very first Anatomy and Physiology class I ever took. I sat right up front because I loved to watch the doctor take his colored markers and draw the capillary. He drew the capillary every class for an entire semester. He would talk about how the capillary had certain ingredients in it: plasma/serum and cells.

Throughout the semester, he went over the importance of each individual part of the capillary and how they all had a specific job or "function" and that we would learn about how each part "functioned." He spoke about homeostasis, how the body is meant to be in perfect balance, and that it is built to keep balance. He also spoke about what happened and how the body responded when a "foreign body" broke through the protective barrier.

It became apparent to me once my eyes were opened up that I was, in fact, infected. Something had gotten in, broken through my barrier, and infected me. Why? How? I thought I was protected. I think the most confusing part to me is that if I was a Christian, going to church, praying, studying the Bible even, how is it that, all of a sudden, I felt different? I actually felt the presence of the Holy Spirit within me. I did not know how to explain this to anyone around me. So, I just kept learning and growing. I became aware of my *need* for God, Jesus, and the Holy Spirit.

I became obsessed with all things Bible, sermons, and worship music. I started to turn off the world and turn on the Father, Son, and Holy Spirit. The more I filled myself up, the more it overflowed out of me, but also the more I realized that I was not only wrong about so much, but I was way, way, way wrong about so much. I was being isolated from the world on purpose. God's purpose. He has a purpose for each and every one of us. We can choose to be close to God and fulfill His purpose from a young age. Or we may have to go through some wandering in the desert like the Israelites. I just hope that you won't wander for forty years like I did.

Once I realized that I was infected, I had to think about all that was infecting me. The areas in my life that I had allowed the world to enter into my soul and try to take over my mind. There is a great book written by Caroline Leaf called *Switch On Your Brain*, which I had read a few years prior to this isolation. I learned from that book that we have a thinking mind, a brain. It stores information the way we remember it. The thing is, we store emotions and feelings as well as the sights, smells, and things we hear. Each and every memory that we store is specific to us and only our memory. Every other person will remember the exact same situation from their perspective. This is something that I have had to learn to come to respect in myself and in others.

The thing is, we often remember the way we felt during a situation, and sometimes that feeling is wrong. Or we make up what we "think" someone else "thinks" about a situation or about us and keep that as a memory. The reality is that we often take on the blame and shame for things in our lives that we did not have any control over at all. Think about driving a car, getting into an accident, and harming the other person in a car. You may feel shame and guilt for being the driver, but the reality was that you had no control over the time and space that you were in. With God, there is purpose in all things, although at the time, we may not see it. For a personal example, the chiropractor who injured my back was doing his normal day-to-day job, and then, all of a sudden, my back was injured. He probably adjusted ten people that day alone, but my back just could not take that normal everyday adjustment, and from that point on, my life was not the same.

I was fully aware, with the Spirit in me, of who I was for the first time in my life. I finally felt like I belonged to someone. I now know who I am and who I belong to. This was something that I spent years having agreements with the devil about. I agreed with him that I was not wanted by my parents. Obviously, my mom was on birth control pills. No, that was not true at all. See, it is never that we do not want to reproduce a baby; it is always that we are scared and oftentimes reproduce under sinful situations, so we then feel shame and guilt when we become pregnant. Or we have no money or any way to provide for a child. The one thing that I know for certain is that there is *no human* whose birth is a mistake. We are all the creation of God; He chose our parents and our birth location specifically to fit His purpose for our lives. There is nobody born on this earth who He does not know about. He was present at your Birth, and He will be present when you breathe your last breath. Just like Mary, the mother of God, He chose you to be the carrier of His Holy Spirit. He wants to birth in you His purpose for you so that you can live a full life on earth, just like He always intended for you. As each person chooses to believe that God sent Jesus to die for our sins, we then take on the responsibility of getting to know Jesus.

The more I studied the life of Jesus, the more I realized that I was infected *big time*! I had some pretty crazy beliefs, and as I read the Bible, I realized that not only was I wrong, but I had been way wrong. Jesus walked me through each and every sin and wrongdoing; he showed me all the agreements that I had made with the enemy and wiped my soul clean. He opened up my eyes, just like the blind men in the Bible. I all of a sudden realized how I had been living, that I owed my husband an apology, that I needed to get away from all those he had been warning me about, and that I just would not listen to him. Not only my husband but my mentors and my family had been pushed away.

As I came to the conclusion that I had become infected, I had to take a moment and try to pinpoint where I turned my back on God and why. What was my priority? It is not that I ever fully turned away. When I needed Him, I called for Him. He was always there to answer my questions, to get me the "job,"…or was that a friend? That was definitely always a friend. So, now I see that I never followed Jesus into any of my jobs that pulled me away from going to church on Sundays. At least I grabbed my values once a week before I graduated from nursing school. I had to ask myself hard questions about what I was doing with my life and surrender fully to being cleansed and restored.

It just makes sense if I use the obvious to explain to you the nature of disease by using a "virus." See, the thing about a virus is initially, when it gets into our body, it takes time for it to reproduce and be visible to others. You will walk around infecting those around you and be totally unaware that you are even infected. Isn't this what we always do? We start to hang out with new people, get a new job, join a new church, or maybe start working out at a new gym. Now you are in a new environment, around a new association, and before you know it, they break through the skin first. Then, they seep into your veins. Before you know it, you are one hundred percent infected by the association you are surrounded by.

The thing was that I had to be physically removed from this environment by God. Have you ever had a parent grab your arm and pull you away from danger? Or reach in and save you from drowning in a pool? Think about the storm in the Bible. I was just reading in Mark 4:35–41 that Jesus was in the boat during a "furious squall," and He was sleeping. Jesus does not get infected by what infects us. We allow any and all storms to infect us; they come into our lives and take them over. Jesus was aware of the storm and was just going to let it blow over.

We have got to learn how to place ourselves in an environment and not become of the environment.

Accepting Christ as my Lord has allowed me to see a storm coming and know that because I have placed Him at the center of my heart and soul and His Spirit has taken over my life, in any storm, I can just sleep on a cushion, and everything is going to be okay. That does not mean that the boat is not going to end up with some damage, but that we are going to learn how to be stronger than we were before the storm. If we allow it, we will learn a lesson from the storm that we can use to help someone navigate in the future. The storm is not even always about us. Maybe we are going through the storm just so we can meet someone through the storm that we are going to help, or vice versa.

Let's go back to how we became infected for a minute. We were enveloped and taken over by the pathogen. We try to fight back at first, but sometimes our bodies just can't fight off the pathogen, and it can take us over locally or systemically. If the infection stays local, we still treat it from the inside out, so no matter how you become infected or how bad the infection becomes, the treatment is from the inside out. If you were exposed to a pathogen, it will also depend on exposure time and the amount of pathogen that you initially became infected with. Any foreign substance that comes into our bodies, no matter how it enters it, will have an instant effect on our bodies, mind, and spirit. We must be constantly aware of our association and input. Once we become infected, it is only a matter of time before the infection that started on the inside works its way externally, and the people around you will start to notice that something is different in you and that you have changed.

Change is not always a bad thing. Depending on why you are changing, it can be a good thing. The thing to focus on is, what are your inputs and associations? This is what infected you, to begin with. You inserted yourself into a new association and started to take in the surrounding input until a small change started to take over. Eventually, you are completely infected by your new input and association, and nobody who used to know you recognizes you. Now, what do you do?

I can tell you what happened to me. I became infected with a new association of friends who were all headed in the same direction as me or stuck in the same misery as me. I graduated from college and focused all of my attention on working for the weekends and partying every chance I got. I thought that I was healthy, though, because I was working out and dieting, so I was "healthy," right? It did not matter that all of the people that I was associating with were partying all weekend, too, and all going nowhere but into debt fast. I was following down those same steps. Our mentor talks constantly about how if you have five loser friends, you are the sixth.

You can't mix sugar in a glass of water and have part of the water stay unsweet. That is what happens when you mix someone who has the Spirit in them with someone who is not filled with the Spirit; we start to dilute what we find acceptable and not acceptable. Before you know it, everything becomes acceptable, and nothing is off limits, and there are no boundaries in your life. This is a dangerous place to end up. We want to live this life with no consequences, but the reality is that life is not easy and will never be easy, and every decision comes with a consequence. Jesus reminds us that

"…in me you may have peace. In this world you will have trouble. But take heart! I have overcome the world" (John 16:33). Jesus is the antibiotic, the anti-inflammatory, the antidote to any ailment that we may be facing. He is the one that heals us from being infected.

How does He heal us, you may be asking? He heals us by coming into our lives and cleansing us with His love and forgiveness. He enters into our soul and goes into every single part and clarifies the junk that has entered us without our knowledge or permission. We have people come in and out of our lives, and they cause damage; some of us feel that this damage cannot be repaired. Jesus can heal the most infected soul. You will not, can not ever be so infected that Christ Jesus cannot cleanse you. There is nothing in this world that He has not come into this world to eradicate. There are no diseases that He has never heard of, no sin he has not cleansed before. There is nothing too bad or perverted for Him to repair. He knows everything you have been through. He has seen each and every moment of your life. He has felt each pain with you.

He has heard all the things that have been

said about you and to you. He has watched every time someone hurt you, and every time they hurt you, they hurt Jesus too. You were never alone in receiving the pain. You are never alone in receiving pain. You will never be alone when receiving pain. Jesus has already gone ahead of you, and the Spirit of God is right inside of you, softening each and every blow you take. Let Jesus come into your soul and fix all the things that you have got wrong. Let Him run through your mind, body, and soul and wash away your sins. Let Jesus clean out your blood and wash you clean. Let Him remove the blood that you were born with and replace it with His blood. Let Jesus give you a new life full of the Holy Spirit, full of joy, love, peace, and happiness.

It took me being physically removed from my association due to illness for me to start taking in my antibiotic and anti-inflammatory. I was infected, inflamed, and mad. We do not even realize that we are also infected with a negative mindset. This is one thing that my new association of people talked a lot about, and that was that changing your mindset from negative to positive is a choice and one that must be intentional.

Our input weighs heavily on our emotions and what drives us to act the way we act. Once I was physically removed from my job, I had to take an honest inventory of what my input was. Who/what was I listening to? Who/what was I reading? Who/what was I watching? Who/what did I spend physical time with? Who/what was I talking and conversing with? Where was I getting my news? All of these things matter, but I never paid much attention to what they were. I did not realize that it was shaping my character. I realized that I needed to make a change if I ever wanted to live a life that was characterized by Christ. Once you realize that you are infected and you start taking your antibiotic, then you become aware of where you need to make changes in life. Your eyes become open to your input and how inappropriate it is, and you will start to make necessary changes. Once you are called to be a follower of Christ, you have no choice but to start to make the necessary changes. If you do not, that is basically like not taking your antibiotics. The infection will flare back up, worse than it was before. You have to continue inputting The Father, Son, and Holy Spirit all day long, each and every day.

CHAPTER 7:

I/A

One day, I was sitting in a meeting, and our mentor drew on the board "I/A." I sat there and thought about where I had seen that before. I realized that in veterinary medicine, it was very common to write on the board "I/A" whenever a dog or cat came in with an abscess. An abscess is an infection that has built up locally and usually causes a large, gross wound that has to be "irrigated and aspirated," and that is why we wrote "I/A" on the board. The wound has to be opened up or aspirated to get the infection out and then irrigated with liquid to flush out the infection. I had to stop and see that the treatment for our input and association is, in fact, to irrigate and aspirate our input and association. We have to completely suck it out and then wash it out.

Think about a glass of water again. If you place a cup of sugar in thirty-two ounces of water, how much water would it take to rinse all the sugar out of the glass and the water to just be plain water again? It will take an unknown amount of water to dilute out the sugar you placed in the cup. Our lives are no different, and oftentimes, God must physically remove us from our input and association to start the dilution process. Some of us are not strong enough to get away from our input and association, and unfortunately, for those of us who are too weak, God will remove us by force.

I was the type of person whom God had kept removing for short periods of time from my input and association, and I was able to slowly change my daily input. As I changed my input and association, the old input and association started to rub me the wrong way. I found that as I was changing each and every day, certain behaviors in me and others that I found acceptable before, suddenly I could not tolerate around me anymore. It was not that they had to change to be around me; it was more that I did not feel comfortable being around them anymore. I started to see patterns in those around me that I found unpleasant. The thing was, those were traits or habits that I also had. For example, spending hours binging a TV show and not thinking twice about the fact that the input was changing my mind and how I thought and felt about the world around me.

God was not only changing my input and association, but He also started me down a path that ultimately will lead to full and total restoration of my mind-body spirit. As I sit and write this now, I am two weeks post-op from a surgical repair that has ended the nightmare that I felt like I was living. When you are in what feels like a nightmare and have no one person to whom you can turn, you learn a lot about yourself if you choose to stop and see what is infecting you. I was in such a situation that I had no choice but to stop and look inward and upward. God was the only one with the answers that I needed, and for what felt like an eternity, I lived in what felt like a nightmare at first, until I changed my input and association.

I read a quote in Dave Ramsey's book, *More Than Enough*, where he quoted a preacher named Chuck Swindoll, who said, "God answers all prayers. His answers can be yes, or no, or grow. Sometimes, your heavenly Father sees you in the fire and, like that goldsmith, allows that boiling action to clean impurities from you. When He looks into the gold (you) and sees His image a little clearer, He douses the fire. Never fear that the fire can be too hot, because He has His hand on the thermostat." I can relate to that because I felt, for the past few years, like I, too, have been held under extreme pressure to clean my spirit. I did not want to admit that I was so infected with a negative mindset that it had taken over my soul. I fed off of any and all negativity, and I did not even realize that I had become the worst version of myself. I had allowed myself to become infected with the world and needed to have a complete irrigation and aspiration of the world, but how? How do we remove the world that we have to live in? Sometimes, God does not allow us to figure that out. I did not know this at the time, but I was predestined to undergo exactly what happened to me.

In 1 Peter 1:1–2, Peter says, "To God's elect." God elected us, "who have been chosen according to the foreknowledge of God the Father, through the sanctifying work of the Spirit, to be obedient to Jesus Christ and sprinkled with his blood." God not only elected/chose us, He did it before we were ever born. He knew that we would eventually become obedient to Jesus in our lifetime and have the Spirit sanctify us. These are all gifts given by God. I personally was unaware that I had been chosen, but I felt a calling and a pull that was undeniable prior to my back being broken and my life being taken over by a health challenge. I had always felt called, but I never felt like I was in a place to contribute. In every job I ever had or task given, I felt like I was not being used to my fullest potential, but I never even knew what my potential was.

See, when we are lacking the Spirit, we are not even our complete selves. God has preordained each and every one of His children. We all know it and feel it within our core. The further we drift from our core of who we are, the more shame and guilt we feel, and the more depressed and anxious we become. We start to live in a season of regret and fear because we are not living in alignment with our spirit. Then, we start to numb ourselves in any way possible. We distract ourselves with work or start using substances to forget. The reality is, though, the Truth is always there; everywhere you go, the Truth is following you, nothing can remove it from you, and you will either seek it or run from it your entire life.

The thing for me that pulled me away from seeking the Truth and what pulled me out of alignment was becoming a nurse. I was dedicated to studying and learning more about Christianity and the character of Jesus while I was in school, but the second I graduated from college and started to work as a nurse, I shifted my schedule and started to work on Sundays. I told myself that I needed to make money, and because I was a new hire, I had to take the worst shifts available. I was the last person to pick my shifts each month, so I got stuck working Sundays. Of course, that is no excuse to completely drop the Bible, church, and prayer, but that is exactly what I did. My family followed whatever I did because I led our family, so everyone quit going to church.

This is where you do not realize the control that you have over your family until you look back and see the choices that you make and how they affect others around you. I was focused on myself and taking care of my patients now, and the way I would contribute to my children now was financially. They all seemed perfectly fine with this new agreement, and we all turned away from God and church; I can only speak for myself, though. I turned away from all of it. I started to turn to my "friends and family" when I needed advice or help with any life circumstances, and I started to increase my debt and increase my time away from my family. I would go from one job working three days a week to three jobs working five to seven days a week. I was making more money than ever, and my debt was increasing faster than ever. I didn't even see the hole I was falling into, and neither did anyone else. I was not only working too much, but we had started working out intensely; I had become addicted to working out (CrossFit, weight training, and yoga), and we had dedicated all our spare time to working out and dieting.

I thought that I was on the right path, but God knew that I had veered off course, and that is when He took over by starting my journey with a phone call. From that day on, my course would change, and I would be placed on a path of discovery laced with pain so deep. I would spend three years on my hands and knees each and every day, tears streaming down my face, begging God to end my suffering. I did not care how; I just could not handle the pain anymore. Then, the next day, I would wake up, and the pain would still be there. I would beg and plead to God to end my suffering, day in and day out, day in and day out, day in and day out. The next day, I would wake up, and the pain would still be there. This was a cycle I would be stuck in for years. To this day, I am in pain, but I know that we are all in pain each and every day. Pain is an indicator; pain has a purpose. P.A.I.N. is Patiently, Aligning, Internal, Negativity. Anytime we have pain, who are we upset with? God, right? God is positivity, and the world is negativity. Pain is directly related to something negative in our lives. We must take all negativity and find a way to turn it into positivity. God specializes in turning negative situations into positive outcomes.

As soon as I started to walk towards God and close the doors to the enemy, that is when the pressure started to increase. It isn't until we start to put up boundaries in our lives that the enemy will begin to attack. When we live in harmony with the world, the enemy will refresh us. Anytime we are hungry, the world will supply a delicious snack. When we are thirsty, the world will quench our thirst. The problem is that what the world offers will never satisfy us, and our flesh will desire more the second we are hungry or thirsty again, and we will never fill up. As we pour the world's food and drink in, it leaks out of the holes that we have, the holes we are trying to fill with the world's meals. The Truth does not leave us wanting or needing more; in fact, often, when we hear the Truth, it makes us sick to our stomachs. The Truth makes us feel as if we just got punched in the gut. There are many times in the Bible where food is referenced, and we all know that it is related to input and association. What we take in is what we pour out. I never realized that the input that I was feeding myself was, in fact, poisoning my soul (mind, will, and emotions).

It was not until I was physically removed from my input and association that I was finally aware that I was hurting myself just by my input and association. God was "aspirating" me from my association and input one surgical procedure at a time. It started first with an eight-week leave for my first neck surgery, followed by three months off for lower back surgery. Then it was another few months off for another neck surgery...then, I was removed for good. When you are isolated, like we all were during the pandemic, you will start to question if you are being isolated for your protection from others or their protection from you. Everyone's truth for themselves is just that, personal. God will reveal in His timing why you are in isolation. He is strictly looking for a heart posture during this time.

When Peter was introduced to Jesus and began following Him, he did not hesitate to take Jesus into his home and introduce Him to his ill mother-in-law. In Mark 1:29–31, Jesus went to Simon's mother-in-law, took her hand, and helped her up; the fever left her, and she began to wait on them. This is the power that adding Jesus to our association has on each of us. The second we accept Christ and allow Him to live within us, we are responsible for introducing Him to all of the people we know who are sick, hurting, and in need of healing. Jesus did not come to heal the healthy but the sick. We are all hurting or sick in one way or another; it's just that some of us hide our pain better than others. We are responsible for being like Peter in the passage and bringing Jesus to those in need of His love.

Today, we understand that illness is not directly linked to sin, but when we come to understand more about sin, we can see that the choices we make where sin is concerned do have consequences that we have to live with. Sin is not to punish us; it is to protect us. We do not put a fence around our yard to keep intruders out. Typically, we put a fence around our yard to keep things from getting out of the yard, such as children or animals. This is what boundaries are for. We have boundaries in place to protect us from harm. Call it a boundary or call it sin, it still has a purpose, and that is protection. We must accept at some point in life that the choices we make come with blessings or consequences, and as we live, we learn.

As I was being pressed, I was trying not to let myself off the hook. When we get injured, or someone hurts us, we often want to stop and look at the past and dwell on what was and then get sad about what will never happen that we had put all our hopes and dreams into. This is what happened to me as I started to lose feeling in my hand, and I was only a few short years into being a nurse. I have $100,000 in student loans to pay back. I just started working as a nurse and paying those loans back a few short years ago, and now I literally can't hold on to a piece of paper because I can't feel it between my fingers. I was watching my future fade away, and everything that I had spent years working toward was being stripped from me.

All I have known since 1999 is being a nurse. I have woken up for the past twenty years and known that I needed to get up and get to work because someone's animal or someone needed me to come and take care of them. I had what I felt was a strong purpose. A God-given purpose. So why is all of this happening to me? As my life started to change rapidly, I had an anchor to hold on to. In November of 2019, I started to get serious about changing my input and association. My mentor became my rock, and my Lord and Savior became my anchor. I was facing the most excruciating pain day in and day out, and I continued to press into the new association. They were teaching me to align my life with my values and how to live with the ultimate purpose for God and for the love of His people.

We all understand what it feels like to have someone come into our lives and completely change them if you have ever made a new best friend or fallen in love. There are times when people come into our lives, and it is not in a positive way; there is a car accident, or you endure a tragedy together. New people come into our lives each and every day if you leave your house. The question is, are they there for a moment, for a reason, for a season, or for a lifetime? I believe that each person we encounter is an opportunity to positively or negatively affect the other. I also believe that God is watching us to see if we will reflect His love onto one another. Each person we encounter provides an opportunity for us to show God's love to His children. Sometimes, that love feels good, and sometimes, that love hurts. The Truth is not always something we want to hear, but it is always something we need to hear. The Truth comes directly from the creator of it, and that is God. The only way to know His truth for your life is to get to know Him. The only way to get to know God is by reading His words, which are written in the Holy Bible, to pray, and to commune with other believers.

Personally, I was so confused. I am a nurse, and I honestly did not understand what was happening to my own body. My spine was deteriorating rapidly, and with each and every bite and drink, I was taking a punch to the gut. I am also very sure that everyone around me thought that I was just crazy and having issues because of my back and neck. I had every nurse, doctor, friend, and relative giving me their opinion and advice about what my diagnosis was, but the truth was they were all wrong. Psalm 139:13–16 says,

> *For you created my inmost being; you knit me together in my mother's womb. I praise you because I am fearfully and wonderfully made; Your works are wonderful; I know that full well. My frame was not hidden from you when I was made in the secret place, when I was woven together in the depths of the earth. Your eyes saw my unformed body; All the days ordained for me were written in your book before one of them came to be.*

I had to keep telling myself that even though all the doctors were telling me that I did not have anything wrong, they were wrong, very wrong. I know my body, and God knows my body. I did not have any issues eating before my lower back surgery; for crying out loud, I was obese. For a year, I would go to the doctor, and they would say that my back was not the issue, and my stomach and GI were not the issue. I would leave the doctor crying, frustrated, feeling hopeless, helpless, and useless.

There comes a time in a chosen child of God when you will be isolated due to infection. You will feel alone. You will have a pressure so heavy that you will feel like you are being crushed from the inside out. I was feeling this internal pressure, and it was an actual physical pressure. My mind (soul), my body, and my spirit were all being held under extreme pressure. I did not have anyone I could turn to who understood what I was going through. The way people looked at me with doubt and skepticism. I could tell some people felt sorry for me; they pitied me. I could feel the stares at my body as it slowly started to lose all the fat. People started to see the muscle under the fat that

I had built for years and actually thought I looked amazing. Everyone judged my exterior and my story. I mean, why wouldn't they? I was shrinking before everyone's eyes, and they could all "see" the change. I just did not have an explanation as to what was happening. All I had who would listen was God. My input started to change and focus first on God and His purpose for my life. I did not know what that was, but I knew that I had to die to myself and accept that I was not here on this earth to fulfill my purpose. I was put here to fulfill *His* purpose, and that is to spread *His* love. His love is so perfect and what we all strive to reach. We are all searching for something, and that something is Him. We all have a hole in the core of our spirit that needs to be filled, and it is shaped in the form of our Lord and Savior, Jesus Christ. As soon as Jesus opened my eyes and allowed me to see what I was living for, all I wanted to do was fill my spirit up with His perfect and overflowing love.

I had to start changing my input and association, and that would be anything I listened to, read, watched, and anyone whom I allowed time with. Acts 4:20 became a theme in our lives: "As for us, we cannot help speaking about what we have seen and heard." I realized that the Holy Spirit works exactly like a cell phone. When we are born, we are given the phone (Holy Spirit); our parents are responsible for charging the phone (Spirit) and keeping it updated and functioning until we reach a certain age, and then we start to make our own decisions in life. We then become responsible for charging the phone. If we want time with the Spirit, we then need to charge the phone (Spirit), keep the content appropriate, and keep it up to date. This is where we all fall prey to the world and the negative forces that are in it.

Once we stop listening to our parents and start listening to ourselves, this is where we become vulnerable to our own desires. This is when flesh takes over, and all of our desires become carnal. Our desires become what fulfills us and what satisfies our flesh. We see it, we want it, we have got to have it now. Our phones give us access to everything we could ever want at a faster pace than ever. What happens when you have the answers at your fingertips but still come up empty-handed? What do you do when there is nothing to order online to solve your problems? What do you do when you can't eat to satisfy the ache you feel in your core? What do you do when you feel like the pressure is too much to take?

When I started the chapter, I was talking about an abscess. They get so big and firm that the infection causes a rupture of the skin and more damage to the outer body. The goal is to treat the infection by aspirating and irrigating the infection. This is exactly what we must do with our input and association; we must do a total inventory, get out the bad, and replace it with good. Some people may think this is too extreme. Jesus literally told His disciples that they should leave everything, sell everything, and follow Him. Is it extreme that when you make a decision to live for Christ, He would expect you to get rid of all old input and associations that He would not approve of? What do those things consist of? If you would not do it with Jesus sitting next to you or would not share what you are inputting with Jesus, then *stop*! You do have to start to get to know the character of Christ by spending time with Him. Read the four gospels of Mark, Matthew, Luke, and John; read them repeatedly if you must until you start to understand the character of Christ. Then, you will have to do what every disciple has to do: become disciplined. It is a word that nobody likes: discipline.

I am not saying that each and every person reading this is going to want to become a disciple of Christ. I am sharing my testimony, what I went through, and what God has taken me through. This is not a play-by-play of what you need to do. This is what I went through and the lessons I learned along my journey toward living with purpose.

There are different levels of injury, illness, infection, and diseases that come into our lives. We will all be affected by pain in one way or another. God is always watching, always present in your life, always rooting for us to rise up and show His love to others. When we are in pain and suffering, this is when we have God's full attention. He never lets us suffer alone, so He is right there with you, taking on the pain, and the way people treat you and you treat others shows a lot about your character. God will use these times of pressure to grow your character and to see how you will react. Let's all agree that nothing surprises God. He knows all things; He is just waiting for us to catch up to the path He has laid out before us. Oftentimes, we are too distracted by the world to see the path that Jesus is lighting up for us. We accept the darkness and run from the light…why? Shame and guilt? Some will tell you it is shame and guilt. I think for a lot of people, it is a lack of education today. We are educating our society to accept sin and to market it. We do not market and sell what is actually going to happen to people when they follow the world's path and ignore the path that God has laid out for us. This is when disease sets in, and darkness overtakes us, but we all have a choice. God is watching to see what you will choose; will you choose to eat from the tree of "knowledge of good and evil" or the tree of "life"?

Romans 8:6 (KJV) reads, "For to be carnally minded is death, but to be spiritually minded is life and peace." I had never known peace. I had never understood what it meant to live in peace. My life had always been carnally minded. We can live our lives trying to understand all the reasons why people are good and bad, or we can eat off the tree of life and put all of our trust in God. I decided that I was going to submit my life to God. I was going to eat from the tree of life for the rest of my life. I was going to become a disciple of Christ. On July 4th, 2021, after a year and a half of exploration of myself, I accepted my faults, I repented of my sins, I knew that I did not want to live one more day not being disciplined in my flesh and faith… so I was water baptized. From that day forward, I have felt the presence of the Holy Spirit living and dwelling within me. I make sure that I am charging my phone (spirit) daily and keeping all my hardware and software up to date. I will never be caught without a fully charged Spirit again!

Shortly after I was baptized, the local churches started to open back up, and I was excited to start searching for a church body that we could grow in. The first church we started attending was a big non-denominational church. The music was great, but the pastor was hard to get close to. I was looking for a pastor, someone to steward me into discipleship. Unfortunately, I did not find any footsteps to follow in at that church. I had been watching a few local pastors online, and there was one in particular I liked, but his church was as far across town as possible. After our mentors started inviting us to said church, we decided to make the drive one Sunday and have been parishioners ever since. We have bonded with the pastor and believe he will help steward us into discipleship, as well as be amazing examples for others to follow.

We had the privilege of sitting down with the pastor, and then with him and his wife for one-on-one meetings. I was able to discuss not only our life dynamic but also our church dynamic, our relationship with the Trinity, and our current mindset, and we began a prayer group amongst us. As soon as the pastor and his wife started to pray for me, I felt things shifting in my world, as if prayers were finally starting to be answered. One of the answers that was finally answered was a diagnosis, or so I thought. I, finally, was given a diagnosis of what was causing this suffering. I was diagnosed with a vascular disorder that was causing my *dis*-ease.

CHAPTER 8:

Disease

Going through the diagnostic process is quite exhausting nowadays. There are so many tests that can pinpoint a problem, but very few disorders get diagnosed these days, and even fewer disorders that are not at least treatable with medications. So when I started to go through the diagnostic process, and no doctor could diagnose me, I began to not only think I was crazy but feel crazy. Not only was my body at disease, but my mind was at disease, and the only thing I had going for me was that my faith was strong. I plugged in tighter to my faith during this time in my life than ever before. Disease, when broken down...dis- is the opposite or absence of, so disease is just the opposite or absence of ease; therefore, anything that is not easy for us automatically places us in dis-ease.

For one full year, I had undergone every GI test in the book, and each one came back perfect.

I knew one thing, and that was that my issue was not my GI tract; I had to move on, and so did my neurosurgeons. They also had to accept that my GI was not the issue, but they still refused to fix my back. I was fighting with each and every doctor by this point. They wanted to pump me with medication that I refused to take. I wanted them to diagnose me. I refused to take any medication until they diagnosed me with something.

The only thing I had at this point was my faith, my closest family members, and my mentors. It is when your input and association get completely uprooted that God can finally start to fix what we broke. I was at dis-ease in every sense of the way. My whole life was being uprooted and flipped upside down. Everything I thought I knew was about to get turned around. Jesus was about to change everything I ever thought and make it *His*.

Dr. P referred me to Dr. M. You know God works in mysterious ways. The entire time I was enduring the pain, God was making major shifts in the people who would play huge roles in my diagnosis. The two doctors who diagnosed me together both moved to Las Vegas right after I was baptized. I had an appointment scheduled with my normal neurosurgeon (Dr. G), who had performed three spinal surgeries on me and then walked in Dr. P.

Dr. P introduced himself to me and then went over my results. He told me that there was a "hot spot" at T9-T10 and that he wanted me to have a block; he referred me to Dr. M because he believed I had a vascular disease called Superior Mesenteric Artery Disease (SMA). He wrote down the diagnosis and sent me on my way. This obviously got my mind working overdrive. By this point, I had already been led down so many paths of possibility that I refused to accept any diagnosis. I was intrigued and willing to go meet with Dr. M.

As everyone knows, the waiting time between the "you may have…" to the tests, to the actual diagnosis, to the treatment can be just as agonizing as the problem itself. The waiting and the not-knowing get our minds moving in all directions. When I was living in these times, I had already established a daily routine. The way to take control of your mind is to keep it active. I learned this when I was a child, and I was neglected and left to myself a lot. I figured out very quickly as a child that I could open up a book and go on an adventure, a new one every day.

I think back to when I was a child; one of the big movies of the day was *The Never-Ending Story*. The story came alive in the child's imagination so much that he just read and read and read a day away. That was me as a child. I didn't even mind being alone and neglected; I really think I preferred it, just like I do today. I liked having my alone time with my imaginary friend (Jesus), reading, dancing, singing, stretching, imagining, playing, and just being me, just like today. Reading was very therapeutic for me as a child, and my child-like intuition was to reach for a book, but not just any book, *the Book*. The only Book that will pass from this life to the next. The Book of His story. The Book of our lives. The Holy Bible. The living, breathing breath of God. It is God-breathed. It is the Word of God, the Truth of God, and our reality. I picked up His Book, and it just came alive during this time for me.

I locked myself in my room, and I started to live day in and day out W.O.R.K.I.N.G (Worshiping Our Risen *King* In New Growth). I shrunk down my input and association and locked in on God. I felt an overwhelming compulsion to be in *His* presence. I was starving physically because of the pain I felt with each bite and drink, but I was being fed by the power of the Holy Spirit. I read how Jesus went forty days with no food, and I could somewhat sympathize because I had to give up most of the foods I liked and live off of very little. I did not endure forty days, and many go without food for more than forty days.

The miracle during that time was that even though I had no energy, when I was home alone, before each outing, I would clean up and fix my hair, put on a fresh face and a smile, and unless you knew "me," you would not have known I was so sick. I understood what it was like to be "tempted" by food. Most food was eliminated from my diet a year prior to this diagnosis, and I had resorted to only eating supplements and minimal food; I was practically a well-oiled machine when it came to diet at this point. The problem was other people around me and the judgment placed on the diet I was "choosing."

Diet is so crucial in our lives. We are what we

eat and drink. I know there are so many diet fads out there, and they change every other day, but as a nurse and someone who has had food challenges my entire life, I believe we are what we eat. Our bodies can easily get thrown into disease when we are not eating properly. God has created us in such a way that we maintain balance, but when you start to get off balance because you get off the path of life, then God may have to knock you down, and that is when disease comes in. God can keep us from harm, but if we continually choose wrong, eventually, He will allow us to get taken down.

I booked an appointment with Dr. M and started to do a little research on SMA, and I was having my mind blown. I 100 percent had all the symptoms, and the treatment was a balloon placement in an artery. I was feeling optimistic that even if I was diagnosed with a "disorder," it could be repaired, and I would be restored back to full health.

Dr. M and I shook hands, and he looked right at me and said, "You have MALS (median arcuate ligament syndrome)." No hesitation, no doubts about it. He actually said, "You do not have SMA; you have MALS." Then he looked it up on his phone and let me read about it while he stepped out of the room. He came back in and looked through all the tests and papers I brought in, and we talked about my history of pain in my abdomen and issues with pain when I ate as a child. He told me that he would need to assemble a team so that we could surgically repair the issue, but he needed two diagnostic tests performed first. I needed to get a celiac plexus block and an ultrasound/fluoroscopy-guided arteriogram. They would test the blood flow through my celiac artery during the arteriogram during inhalation and exhalation.

People with MALS will have impingement of blood flow through the celiac artery during exhalation, occluding blood flow to the spleen, stomach, and liver. The one thing that is not tested is people after a meal because these tests are dangerous for a non-fasted person. So many of these tests will not be accurate. The test would only show a true positive impingement if the patient had food or drink in their stomach because that is when the occlusion and pain occur in most patients. There is also a nerve component to this disease where the celiac nerve root/ganglion nerve root is also impinged. The celiac plexus block will either eliminate or relieve pain temporarily, and that would lead to a possible MALS diagnosis as well. MALS is a disease diagnosed only through exclusion, meaning you have been tested and are negative for all other ailments. I was sent home with a probable diagnosis and a plan of action. It was amazing; I had hope again.

During the diagnostic process, I slipped on the stairs and fell. That fall dislocated my right shoulder and broke my last neck repair. This would slow me down and all progress toward being healed because I needed to take care of my shoulder. It would end up needing surgery. I went from being in pain when I ate and drank and sat too long to *Everything hurts all the time*! This is where I felt like I was at rock bottom!

Disease was all I knew for a while, but I had no choice but to keep on pressing forward. God was breaking me down, and I just could not understand what I was supposed to be learning. I would sit up at night and try to figure out what was going on in my body. Doctors were telling me they had never had a patient like me before. I didn't even know what that meant. I refused to take their prescription medications for one, and then I never complained about my issue; I just wanted to fix it. Doctors these days are all about treating a symptom with a pill and never getting to the root of the problem. So, I had to study the root of the problem in me.

When did the disease begin? What was the root cause? Why me? Why can't I just be back at work, taking care of people? That was a good job. I was helping people. I spent ten years getting a bachelor's degree in nursing and did not even walk across a stage to accept a diploma because of the lockdown in 2020. Now, I can't eat, work out, work, drink, sleep, or take care of myself. I felt useless. So why would God be breaking me down? At that point in my life, I had no idea; now, I can say it is because I surrendered. I fully committed and surrendered to God. I told Him I would follow Him and be a vessel for Him to use. *But I was not clean*! I needed to be restored and cleaned.

I was reading Genesis 3:6. I was focused on the word "consumption" and what we eat. In the Bible, when the woman saw that the fruit of the tree was good for food, pleasing to the eye, and also desirable for gaining wisdom, she took some and ate it. She also gave some to her husband, who was with her, and he ate it. Notice "he ate it…" Genesis 3:7 says, "Then the eyes of both of them were opened, and they realized they were naked; so, they sewed fig leaves together and made coverings for themselves."

Consumption. Whatever we are conned into feeding ourselves day in and day out is what we feed the people around us. We are a pump, and the question is, what are we pumping out? I had gotten to a point where I could hardly take in any food, and I had completely started to wash out my input and association. I guess I should just say God did. As I was being diagnosed and unable to be around my normal friends and family, they started to stop calling and checking on me. I was too sick to call and worry about anyone else. I was so ill, and weak, and broken.

All I wanted was to be with God, in the presence of God, hearing God's word, reading God's word, and listening to someone preach God's word. And the *truth* started to wash me out, purify me. I was being placed under pressure. Deep abiding pressure, the kind of pressure that you feel deep in your chest, nothing can make it stop, it hurts to breathe...that type of pressure. Like being shoved in a sterilizer and having all the disease washed out of you.

As soon as the doctor said I could have MALS, I did have to stop and take a look back at my life. Where did I get knocked off track? There is not even one time. We get knocked off track all the time. We may be on track during the work week, then get off track Friday and Saturday evening, and then get back on track Sunday morning when we grab our Bible and go to church. I am guilty of this pattern of living. Tipping Jesus on Sunday (as my mentor says) and thinking that was an acceptable sacrifice. Disease was bred into me. The more I sat under the pressure of pain and starvation, pain and starvation, day in and day out, day in and day out, the more disease was forced out of me.

How? By Jesus and me having an honest discussion about why I thought the way I did about certain life traumas and circumstances in my life. Pivot points were the ones that we focused on. Moving, break-ups, job changes, and habits that were not in alignment with Him. I started to change my mindset, and the disease started to become uprooted. Jesus became the root that grounded me, and I was able to start building on that root while being buried in the deep, dark place of P.A.I.N (Patiently, Aligning, Internal, Negativity).

When thinking about what separates us from God, we are all born in His image, with the breath of *life* in our lungs. We are all living and breathing Spirits; we are subject to our environment, which composes our input and association. Initially, if we are separated from the Spirit, it is because our own family does this to us. Deep down, we have a seed in us that is in our hearts. The seed does not start to grow until it is watered with the Holy Spirit. The way that God speaks to that seed throughout your life is between you and Him. This is my testimony, my vision, my vehicle; I was driving myself off a cliff, and God caught my car and blew it up. My vehicle stopped functioning altogether. If your car is broken, it is not going to get you from point A to point B, let alone help get anyone else anywhere.

This is where the work started to really take place in my spirit. Jesus came along slowly over time, has taken my life, and showed me that He not only was with me, but He was making everything better all along the way. Most of the time, as a child, we do not even know sin/disease is all around us. We are not subject to punishment for the sin that was committed to us, only the sin we commit to ourselves, others, and God.

In Genesis 3:6, I noticed many things while studying, and I figured that if this is where sin and pain (childbirth) started, then I wanted to understand what I had done that caused me to fall from grace. I noticed that the serpent was "crafty," questioned authority, and confused Eve. I had to start taking a look at myself and at my association. Was I questioning authority? Did I think that I was craftier (smarter) than those in a position of authority? I also noticed that once Eve was confused, she added more to what God had said. I believe this is often where we get into trouble. If we "hear" something, that is it; we need to stop adding and subtracting info.

We ladies are so terrible at this. I am the worst! When my husband tells me that he heard, "Suzy passed away last week," he leaves it at that. Now, if I tell my husband the same thing I "heard" (Suzy passed away last week), I will say, "I heard that Suzy passed away; I bet it is because she had a heart attack. She never took care of herself." Now, that would have been me in the past, and even today, this is something that I am working on. We need to *stop* adding in our predictions, thoughts, opinions, and labels because God is the one in charge of all of it. It doesn't matter why things happen. They do, and it is for our good. We may not see it, but God will work all things for our good.

In Genesis 3:6, I noticed the serpent confused Eve and questioned authority; I had to check myself and my association, and it was time to clean it up. I had convinced myself that it was okay to hang out with the serpent because I was not disobeying authority. I could just chill around the serpent, eat with the serpent, go out and drink with the serpent, and then grab my Bible on Sunday and clean myself. This is good, right? No?

I have never been one to physically question authority. However, in my mind and spirit, I have been questioning authority since I was little. I never understood my authority because they behaved so poorly. My parents were neglectful and abusive, and I had decided I would never treat my kids that way, but isn't that questioning authority? Judging others was something I had told myself not to do. I should accept people because God loves all people, and I could associate with whoever because what they have going on with God is between them and Him. I was not doing myself any favors because not only was I listening to the serpent, but I was allowing him to confuse me and tempt me with all the things of the world. I was allowing food coloring in my water bottle, and I was the one who was stained. I was the sinner; I was the one who would suffer the consequences of my own sin.

I think that we as women do not even consider that we are the ones that our husband comes to for love and information. He provides for us, and we are to take what he gives us and turn it into something useful. He brings home groceries, and we make a meal. He plants a baby in us, and we raise him a family. He gives us a house, and we provide a home. The trouble is that men stopped listening to their wives before they got married. They stopped listening to the "Eve" in their life, their mom, long before they met you. Children are so rarely raised with both a mom and a dad that they do not even start out life seeing the family unit the way God intended. I was no different.

Disease started in the "Garden of Eden" when original sin began. We all fall from the grace of God in our life. I know that I have fallen over and over and over again. Jesus is there to rescue me each and every time I fall. He picks me up, and He listens to me. He is the one who comes along and cleans up the messes that we make with our sin. Our Lord God showed up in the Garden; He did not criticize or condemn Adam and Eve, He simply took their crappy clothes and gave them warm and comfortable clothes, and He moved them. He made sure to provide what they needed for their journey before He sent them on it. But, not before telling Eve, "I will make your pains in childbearing very severe; with painful labor, you will give birth to children."

As I read this, I know that giving birth to children can be literal, and it can be completely a metaphor. Any new and creative idea that we come up with is something new that will be birthed into this world. The enemy will try his hardest to keep us from bringing forth life for God, whether it is a literal baby, a book, or praising God...the enemy is watching for us, and it is our job to fight against the enemy. To smash his head, and to keep pressing forward, eating from the tree of life, no matter how good it is for food, how shiny or wise the other tree will make us. If we have disease in our life, it is up to us to take it to God, so that He can take our sin and make it into something good. Our God is so awesome; even if we are wrong, He makes it right. The only problem is, it requires a death to take place. In order for God to fix what we had done, He had to kill a living creature. Death is what covers our sin. In order for us to survive, we must kill.

When I stop and think of that, it is too much for me to accept. Even a carrot is pulled from its life source and stops growing just for us to eat it and survive. Everything we eat must stop growing and living before we eat it; its life source then becomes a part of us. The death of Jesus became the ultimate sacrifice for all of the Church. Christ was the final sacrifice for you and for me. The moment we allow God to cover our sin with the blood of Jesus, we never have to fear the enemy again. The blood is the cloak that covers us all the days of our lives, and even though each new thing we birth is subject to the enemy, it will never be overtaken by the enemy, because God is with us, protecting and providing, and cleaning up all the messes that we make, day in and day out. I was thinking about the word "Bible..." A bib wraps around our head to protect anything from getting on our bodies. Exactly! The word of God, the Bible, is what God gives us to wrap our heads around...if we can do that and live by it, we *will* be covered all the days of our lives.

I had been making mess after mess for forty-six years by the time I was seeing Dr. M and begging God to heal me each and every day. I was in misery, and nothing would go my way throughout the entire diagnostic process for MALS. During my first exam with Dr. M, I had just had COVID and had lost ten pounds; I literally looked my worst, and it still took him months to schedule the arteriogram. After the arteriogram, the "plug" that was clotting the artery came loose, and I started to bleed out from my femoral artery. The nurse applied direct pressure for thirty minutes. It was the most agonizing thirty minutes of my life. I was literally screaming and crying the entire time. She saved my life, although, at the time, I wanted her to let me die. I could not walk for weeks following that procedure.

I continued to suffer from upper and mid-back pain while I was being treated for a broken shoulder. While my stomach was hurting, my back had been hurting, but it would take another year to diagnose why. I spent an entire year in agonizing pain and thinking about the question that God asked Eve in the Garden…He asked her, "What is this you have done?" From the moment I slipped and fell down the stairs until now, over a year later, I have been asking myself, what did I do? What have I done? What has this entire life been for? What am I doing? I had already surrendered my life to Christ, and I felt like I was losing everything.

I could not even shower or dress myself many times throughout this whole life-crushing process! Why was I the one who felt like I was being crushed? The pressure that I was about to be put under would almost be too much for me to handle. The pressure of being put in and through a sterilization process is crushing. I had to have the disobedience ringed out of me. I started to eat from the tree of life…even though I felt like I was dying. I started to submit my life to Christ, and I started to wash myself with the word of God. The higher the pain and pressure, the more time I spent praying, worshiping, reading, and listening to others preach the word of God. God started to overtake my body and repair me one broken piece at a time.

CHAPTER 9:

Sterility/Pressure

While my mind was being cleansed and renewed by God, my body was breaking down. Now, I was dealing with the pain of a broken shoulder, a broken back, and what felt like an alien in my abdomen, all crushing me from the inside out. I could not wrap my mind around what was happening to me. I was considering that I could have MALS and waiting to get approval from the doctor to have a diagnostic and palliative care surgery. So now I knew for sure I needed three more surgeries; I was never going to help get our business off the ground if I couldn't even get myself dressed. There were days when the pressure was literally too much to handle, but what choice did I have? I would spend all of my time praying and trying to learn from the Bible. I could relate to so many of the prophets who wrote the Bible. I was being trapped, imprisoned in a body I did not even recognize. The life I spent ten years fighting for was slowly ripped away from me. How am I supposed to survive all this pressure? How can anyone survive all this pressure?

I had to remove myself from friends and family by the time I was in this state. Nobody understood what was happening to me, and I certainly couldn't explain something I did not understand either. All I knew was that most foods hurt to eat, and moving my body from outside of my house was not a pleasant task. I isolated myself for my own comfort and safety. I refused to take any medications by this time and used only natural pain relievers and supplements, and even this, I tried to avoid. I felt like I was being taken to the school of hard knocks. Every time I tried to get up, I would get knocked back down. The only thing I had going for me was that I was being scheduled to be fixed.

The problem was that the pressure was just about to begin. The real pain and pressure did not begin until after my shoulder surgery. This is where I really felt like I could take no more, and I started to beg God for forgiveness and mercy. Not a day would go by without crying out to God for mercy and forgiveness. I just had to assume that I was being punished for something I had done. I would reevaluate my life over and over while being held under pressure.

Looking back, I understand why I was being held under pressure, but reading my own words while I was actually under that kind of pressure really makes me proud of myself. Here is that journal entry:

"I was thinking about my situation and how I feel like I am under constant pressure. My physical body feels like it is being held under extreme pressure! There are times when I almost feel like I am going to explode! Maybe like my spirit wants out of my physical body! Why me? Why am I going through this? I heard a pastor say that when you are in a place of hopelessness, and you are asking God, why? Why? Why? Answer yourself, 'For God, and to show His *love* to His children!' Through *this*! Yes, *this* pressure…God *is* going to *help* someone else. Someone *will* be saved through *this* pain! Even if *one* is saved, it is worth it, Lord! Even for *one*! I know this is for *way* more than *one*! Pressure…I was brought by the Spirit to my own experience with pressure and the years I spent dealing with a machine meant to *kill* with pressure! Water, heat, and pressure, all put in a closed container, *kill*! The autoclave is a machine used by the medical community to *sterilize*! It dawned on me that I am, in fact, being autoclaved by God! He has me under pressure with the *pain*, which has me all kinds of inflamed (heat), and He is the Spirit (water) that is cleansing me! Killing all of the impurities that are *in* my body that Satan placed there throughout my life!

Unfortunately, when I was young, I only allowed Jesus to be my savior. I continued to lord over my own life, and that has come with the consequences that I am facing now with the repairing of my body. I believe that I am being fully restored back to what God made me to be. But I have been destroying the life He gave me for forty years. He has been spending the last three years cutting into me to repair all that has been broken, but also to release some of the pressure. Then He is holding me under extreme pressure to *kill* the impurities for good. I know that being held under pressure at times can make us feel like we are going to explode, but the important thing to do is to realize that the pressure we are feeling is so we have nothing external to reach for. He wants us to feel so crushed inside of ourselves that we realize that it is *there inside us* that He exists! There is nothing external that can fulfill us, and when He places us under extreme *soul*-crushing pressure, it is because He needs you to die to yourself and *live* for Him and for others…surrender.

At some point in everyone's life, you will be held under extreme pressure. Life is not easy. It never will be. This is the process we all must take in life to get to the promises that God has for us. We all must be held under pressure in order to be cleansed by the Spirit. Everyone's pressure is unique to them; no two autoclaves are the same. They are each built by God for you, not to *kill* you. So that *you* can *live*. We all get placed in an individual tomb. The question is, what do we come out as? God's children? Or the enemy's angel (messenger)? You will give your life to one or the other. When you're placed under pressure, and you hear yourself asking "Why?" Answer yourself, 'For God, and to show His children His *love* for them.' How do you go through extreme pressure to show His love? By what comes out of you while you are under pressure. He is listening to you…watching you…He is with you. Others are, too, surrounding you, taking care of you, or being taken care of by you; this is where He is observing you. Does He need to turn up the pressure? Are you going in the right direction? Do you need to be rotated? Flipped? The journey depends on our reaction to the life He gives us each and every day."

Jeremiah 9:7 says, "Therefore this is what the Lord Almighty says: 'See, I will refine and test them, for what else can I do because of the sin of my people?'" So, it was because of my sin that I was going through the pain and pressure, but it was also for the sin of whoever reads my testimony. Malachi 3:3 says, "He will sit as a refiner and purifier of silver; he will purify the Levites and refine them like gold and silver. Then the Lord will have men who will bring offerings in righteousness." We must be cleansed and purified in order for the offerings and prayers that we bring to God to count. We must be cleansed and purified of all of our impurities in order for the glory of God to reign upon us. We must be pure and obedient in order for the Holy Spirit to fall upon us and live and dwell within us. Well, obviously, I was very, very, very dirty…because the cleansing process that I had to undergo felt like a sharp and abrupt attack each and every day, all day long.

Zechariah 13:9 says, "This third I will put into the fire; I will refine them like silver and test them like gold. They will call on my name, and I will answer them; I will say, 'They are my people,' and they will say, 'The Lord is our God.'" I have learned that what I thought was a personal relationship with God was not. I had no idea, but I was even more lost than a person who had never heard the gospel of Jesus Christ. I was not only lost, but I was responsible for knowing about the Father and the Son; even worse, I was turning my back on the Holy Spirit. I was refusing to be obedient to the Bible. The Bible that I had spent my entire life reading and studying. I knew what I was reading, but I was not "listening." Listening is an active word. You can not just hear the Word and then do nothing. You must hear the word and then act upon it to activate the word in your life.

Jesus said in Matthew 5:13, "You are the salt of the earth…" That made me think about pressure because salt in our bodies increases and decreases our pressure. So, was I being held under pressure to increase my saltiness? Maybe I had let myself get too bland...bitter, even, because I was full of the world, "...But if the salt loses its saltiness, how can it be made salty again? It is no longer good for anything except to be thrown out and trampled underfoot." If you increase the salt in, your pressure goes up...did you know that the word "salary" comes from the Latin word for "salt"? How funny that as our wages/salary go up at our job, we start to feel like the "pressure" is also increasing.

James 3:11 asks the question, "Can both fresh water and saltwater flow from the same spring?" Of course not. The second the two are joined, they both become salty. So, salt is almost impossible to remove. Once you have come into contact with "the salt of the earth," you are forever changed. Once you are touched by Jesus, He can't be unfelt. The only thing that breaks up the bond of H2O is salt, combined with energy...electrolysis. When we come into each other's lives, it is not just a coincidence. It is because God placed us in one another's lives, to impact and change each other. No meeting is coincidental, and no meeting is random. The thin thread that binds us is necessary for each and every one to reach our destiny. Some of us, though... we need to be held under pressure in order to get back to homeostasis, because we let so many people impact us in a not-so-good way. God will come into your life and clean out your hardened heart. Jesus is the one who takes the blame. He took the punishment at Calvary when He hung on a cross for you and me.

The feeling of being held under pressure led me to also think about the womb and a tomb. When a baby is in the womb, they are in a pressure cooker (so to speak). This is a time of new growth, quick growth, isolation, protection, and refinement. God knows each cell in your body; He puts you together one cell at a time. If He made me, then I had to start to tell myself that He could fix me. Just like the baby in the womb, I had to believe that this was not a time of the end but a time of the beginning. I was going to be reborn after these surgeries. The time that it would take and the pressure that I would have to be held under was the part that I could not control. I would just have to trust in God's perfect timing. This was the most challenging part because each day, I was suffering and being crushed from the inside out.

Even though I was being crushed, I still had hope for my future because I was reading the Bible and allowing God's words to cleanse me, wash me, and make me whole. I allowed the words that God was pulling me toward to lift me up and to lift others around me. I wrote in my journal:

"I am *here*! I am living with the blessing of the Holy Spirit; I am going through a sterilization process, being sterilized from the culture that I let infect me! I am being held under *extreme* pressure for the Glory of God! When He is done sterilizing me, I will be a diamond!"

I had heard a few times in business and in sermons that "there is privilege in the pressure," but to be honest, when you are being held under such extreme pressure, you do not feel like you are privileged; but in the Bible, in James 1:2–4, he states that we should…"Consider it pure joy, my brothers and sisters, whenever you face trials of many kinds, because you know that the testing of your faith produces perseverance. Let perseverance finish its work so that you may be mature and complete, not lacking anything." So, once I read that, I knew that I should be happy. God is going to complete me as long as I choose to be joyful through the pressure. It would be my attitude throughout this time under pressure that would determine the outcome. I was in full control of my actions and my attitudes, and I was going to make sure that I was not punishing the ones around me (if I could help it) because I was under pressure. I was still going to be as supportive to my spouse and partners as possible until my trial was complete.

Numbers 21:1–9 talks about how the people grew impatient along the way…Moses was trying to deliver them out of Egypt, and the people were speaking against God and Moses (their leader). I think it is so important, when you are being held under pressure, to examine the words that you are speaking to others, your spouse, your friends, but most importantly, God. God is only going to judge us when all is said and done in our individual lives. We will not have to answer for any other person's actions and reactions, attitudes, and gratitudes. So, do not allow the pressure to push you back to that which you left to begin with. Pressure is meant to purify you, but you must stay under the pressure to get sterilized. Stay under the pressure, reach toward Jesus, and surrender to Jesus. He will help to release the pressure and, when the time is right, remove the pressure completely.

I am a living testament to God's ability to cleanse, and that is why I can write this book now. I was held under extreme pressure to a point where I obviously felt like I was going to combust. Every individual will face a trial of their own and be held under the pressure that God knows they can handle. Each test that we are given by God is tailored to us. God is not going to put you through anything that you can't survive. The goal is to get each and every one of us to follow suit. To follow Jesus, our mentor, teacher, friend, and example of leadership and servanthood. We should all be seeking Jesus without being held under pressure. The problem is most of us refuse to turn to God for our daily lives unless we are held under pressure. So, if that is the only time God will get your attention…He may keep applying the pressure.

Of course, I had to break the word "pressure" down and allow God to define this word for me since it was something I was feeling so intensely. "Press-" is self-explanatory; the question is who is applying the pressure. "U-" is a pressure that is being applied to you from an outside source. Usually, it is God, but it could be your input and association; just know it is something outside of you. "Re-" to change or repent. God or an outside source will press you until you repent or change. You have to make an internal change to help the pressing cease. This pressure is an external pressing for an internal change. God has something in store for you that you will not be able to maintain unless you change completely.

There is nothing wrong with us; we have not done anything to ruin our lives up to this point. We just have not learned what it is that God wants us to learn in order to move our lives forward. He expects a lot out of us; we think we can make minor changes, and then God will answer all of our prayers. The reason why He says "no" a lot is to protect "us." We are not ready for what we are praying for. You want a baby? You have to be held under pressure and hold that baby under pressure in order to make the necessary changes to be able to care for that baby. Your body has to undergo a complete transformation and be prepared to handle the gift that you will be receiving. It is the same with the Holy Spirit. God will not send down the Holy Spirit to live and dwell within you until the necessary changes are made to your body and your mind. You must undergo a complete renewal of your mind and body. 1 John 3:4–6, "Everyone who sins breaks the law; in fact, sin is lawlessness. But you know that he appeared so that he might take away our sins. And in him is no sin. No one who lives in him keeps on sinning. No one who continues to sin has either seen him or known him." Purify yourself.

Maybe you think you can't handle the pressure? You can't. You absolutely can't handle the pressure, and that is why you need the Lord, our God, to guide and direct you. Jesus needs to come into your heart and clean up your mind, body, and soul. Once you submit to Him, He must come into your life and change everything. Depending on your future will depend on the pressure you are held under. The harder the pressure, the bigger the assignment.

If you feel like giving up, *don't*! Turn to Jesus and allow Him to carry you during this time. You may not only be held under pressure, but you may even be *cut*. Yes, that is right, anyone who enters into a covenant with God will get *cut*: surgery. We all have to undergo circumcision when we decide to follow Jesus.

Once you become a Christian, the purpose you will find is to become more "Christ-like," we are to be conformed to the image of Christ, and the way to do that is to "stamp it:" to apply pressure. "You can't conform to the image of anything without 'pressure,'" says Levi Lusko. So, the pressure is necessary to make the change. John 13:8: "Jesus answered, 'Unless I wash you, you have no part with me.'" God puts His "seal of approval" on you when He puts pressure on you, and you lean into Him. As He continues to press, He is watching our response to the pressure He is applying. He knows exactly what we can handle during our transformation, and each person is different. You can consider being put under pressure as a blessing. You were chosen, and your response should be heavenly.

CHAPTER 10:

Surgery

I had surgery to repair my broken shoulder, and that would slow down everything. I could not lay flat for about six months, so it took forever for me to get the final diagnostic tests for my broken back, so I would just have to deal with the pain of my broken facet at T9-T10 for another year. Dr. P suddenly became leery of cutting into my back because he did not have what he felt was an appropriate image to cut into my back. He told me that my back pain, as a symptom itself, only proves the pain is being caused by my back at 50 percent. Even though a bone scan was "hot at T9-T10," he *would not* be convinced my "back" was causing the pain until he had a "clear" image.

He kept scheduling me for steroid injections, which helped with my back pain a lot...but my stomach pain only for one day. I could eat a big meal without pain on the day of my injection and maybe the following day. That would be what would convince Dr. M that I, in fact, was a candidate for MALS surgery.

Obviously, with all of the surgeries, I continued to question God as to why. Why am I having to undergo all of these surgeries? It just seems like I am getting such a bad deal. I questioned God over and over as to why during all of this. It became clear to me that God had a huge purpose for *me*, just like He does for *you*. Why would He…? Because He knew that I would write *this* book and help to educate others as to why they could be going through a pressing, surgery, and all things too much to handle.

You know, anytime you come to a point where it seems there is not one other human being that gets you…God does. He knows you inside and out. He is the only one who understands your every thought. There is no reason to hide from God, not your feelings, not your lifestyle, not your bad habits. Nothing is too big or bad to discuss with God. He wants you to talk to Him; it is called "prayer." Praying is not some special or magical thing, you must say. It is simply a conversation with your creator. If you never talk to your creator, how do you expect to understand yourself?

Again, I heard a pastor's wife say that your relationship with God is the exact same as your relationship with the Bible. That is super true. The people who I know who do not believe in or study the Bible have little to no understanding or relationship with God. I personally have never met anyone who has "read" the Bible and says they "do not believe" in the Bible. I get that some people can read the Bible and not understand it, and to that I say it is because you have not asked for understanding. You have yourself convinced that you do not understand. God has a way to work, grow, and develop each individual according to their needs and their life. Discernment is given through perseverance.

I truly felt like God was restoring me, one surgery at a time, that each and every surgery was a new covenant with God. Each surgery that I would have would, in fact, repair and renew my mind, body, and spirit; I knew it in my heart and because God had said I was "healed." In my heart of hearts, I felt that even though I was suffering in the worst way, and I felt like the pressure was too much to take, I knew that, as each surgery would come up, I was actually being repaired, renewed, and restored, so I welcomed all the surgeries that would be scheduled.

In Genesis 2, God performed the first surgery on Adam because there was "no suitable helper" for man, and it was not "good" for man to be alone. God caused the man to "fall into a deep sleep," aka "anesthesia," and while he was sleeping, God took one of the man's "ribs" and then closed the place with flesh. Is it possible that God still performs surgery for the same reason? In my case, I would say this is true. God has been cutting me left and right, and each time, I find a renewed strength and purpose within me. With each cut, I am being filled with the Holy Spirit, so I am not alone, and the Holy Spirit is my "helper" and guide. So, each cut still has a purpose.

Obviously, the word "surgery" is not in the Bible, and the only surgery that I can find is the one that God performed on Adam. The only word that is in the Bible that is close to surgery is "circumcision" (incision), which is a procedure that was performed to prove that a covenant was made with God. We may not go through a physical "cutting" with each covenant with God, but God will require you to "cut" whatever is "covering" the sin in your life out of your life. Once you "cut" the covering off, then God can propel you into His victory (History).

Deuteronomy 30:6: "The LORD your God will circumcise your hearts and the hearts of your descendants, so that you may love him with all your heart and with all your soul, and live." We must be willing to cut off or take the sin of our life and circumcise it, which means to surgically remove the cover (sin and shame) from our lives. We do not have to continue to walk in disease. Christ came so that we can enter into a covenant with God. Circumcision is the covenant we make to say we are done! We are cutting sin and shame away. The cover that we keep over us must be cut away so that people can see the real version of you. The one that God intended for you to be before sin came and entered into your life. We do not have to carry the shame around. You can be free.

God wants to join in a covenant with you. God wants to offer you a chance to have your sin removed; just like Adam had to be cut, so do you. God said it was not good for man to be alone… without Him. Sin separated man from God. Jesus is the new Promise. Jesus came some 2,000-plus years ago to break the cycle of sin in each and every person's life. The cycle of sin you were born into is also God-given, passed down through our DNA.

We all must accept God's gift for ourselves. We are given a choice to choose our will or His will, but they both have promises made and promises kept. Once you enter into a covenant with God, Jesus will spend time with you, teaching you and reviewing your life with you. Jesus comes to clean you up, and to change your mindset and character to be like Him. This change is a lifelong endeavor. Jesus will call you, and you will fall deeply in love with Him.

Once you fully submit to Jesus and you are walking in obedience daily with Christ, God will appoint you. When God appoints you, He anoints you with the power of the Holy Spirit. The Holy Spirit will come upon you and will live, and dwell within you, and will stay with you until you are joined with Christ in heaven.

You must be submitted to a decision to be committed to circumcision to stand on mission. Surgery is final. Once you are cut, you have a scar, an outward sign to others around you of an inward decision of circumcision. A sign to those that you "have changed," a scar can't be hidden when you are naked. It can't be covered up when exposed. At some point, your scar will show. You will be exposed. You will answer for your sin. We all do. The question is, do you want to pay now for that sin? Or do you want to live until you die with that sin?

What needs to be cut out of your life? What is keeping you from surging forward? God wants to "cut" out of your life the "things" that are holding you back from fulfilling His purpose in your life, the things that are keeping you and Him apart. You are either a part of God's will for your life, or you are apart from God's will for your life. You are a part of the "Bride of Christ," or you will be apart from the "Bride of Christ." The choice is everyone's to make. You are wanted, but you must go through surgery. You must "cut it out..." *Sin* must be cut away.

Once sin takes root in your life, it must be "uprooted." Sometimes, if the sin is not too deep, the person can grow out of sin by changing their input and association. But most of the time, the root of sin is too deep for that, and some pain will be necessary in order to complete the circumcision process. The way God deals with each of us is individual and specific to what we can handle and the purpose God has for our individual lives. We all have a perfect place with God. Freedom is for everyone. God sent Jesus so *all* can be saved. Will you be a part of His bride or apart from His bride? It is a decision to enter into circumcision. Will you stand for one mission?

God's promise for your life can not be fulfilled until you undergo a circumcision. It is between you and God to decide what must be cut out of your life. Sometimes, you must undergo physical surgery; other times, you are just going to have to cut out an association of people. You may have to cut out a mindset. Whatever you have to "cut out," it *will hurt*. No surgery can be performed without causing pain. P.A.I.N.: Patiently, Aligning, Internal, Negativity. You are going to have a complete mindset shift no matter what, and you will be taken through pain.

Once the covenant has been made, God will

start to perform surgery and remove all of the things in your life that do not fulfill His purpose for you. Oftentimes, that is even removing you from your family. You will try to bring them all with you, but they have to go through their own surgery and their own lifetime experience with God. Everyone must make a personal choice themselves to walk away from sin and enter into a covenant with God. It is a personal choice, and the type of surgery that God performs on you is personal to you. Once you choose Him, surgery will be performed, and a "scar" will be left to prove the choice that you made.

Surgery was performed on me again; I would undergo two surgeries: a laparotomy to temporarily treat the symptoms of MALS, and a facetectomy and decompression of my T9-T10 to repair my back. I would be held under pressure for two years after breaking my back. It would take months and months for me to be able to lay flat to get an "image" that would confirm my broken T9-T10 facet joint. All the while, I knew my back was broken, but the doctor refused to agree with me. I would leave each and every doctor visit frustrated and in pain. God was patiently aligning my internal negativity. I needed to trust that no matter what He was taking me through, it was all for Him and to show me how to better love His children. I knew I was working (Worshiping Our Risen King in New Growth) for God, that He would be using me as a vessel to lead His children to Him and an instrument to speak to them. Once I knew this, I understood why I must be cleansed and held under such extreme pressure. I must be able to sympathize and empathize with His children. I have had to endure many heartaches in life. I do not understand everyone all the time, but I can always sympathize with people and lead them to God and His love for them.

As I was undergoing these last three physical surgeries, I also was undergoing surgery of my mind and Spirit. God was cutting out old ideas that had been placed into my mind by the enemy. When we are in dis-ease, we do not even see all of the lies the enemy is placing in our minds. I had to actually go back through my entire life and remove old ideas that had been placed into my mind from the time I was born. From the first thought that my dad did not want "me," I had to place myself in his shoes for just a moment. He was just not mature enough to handle having me, and he never was. God protected me from that man as much as He could. I had the least amount of time with our dad than my siblings.

One of the hardest days of my life was the day I decided to walk away from my dad and all of his family. I just could not take his abuse anymore. It was all verbal abuse, but being called "stupid like your mom" instead of your name cuts just as deep as any physical punishment. The wounds that were inflicted by my dad were so deep that I am only now recovering from them. I cut my father out of my life at eighteen years old, but I also cut my half-brother out of my life that day. I would not ever see or hear from my brother again. I was devastated on the day I had to walk away from my baby brother. He was the light of my life. He loved me unconditionally, and I loved him unconditionally. I had no idea that the love we shared was so powerful. I did not know that I was walking away from my brother for thirty years.

The process of being cut hurts, and cutting things and people out of our lives hurts deeply. The thing is that if you stay close to an association that is causing your infection or disease, then you have to cut them out. Oftentimes, we do not go under the knife when a covenant is made with God. Some of us have to cut an association of people out of our lives because they are keeping us too close to the sin that is causing our shame and guilt. It is better for you to be cut than to continue to stay in your illness. Some people fear getting cut so badly that they would rather just stay in their sin and shame. They fear more what other men and women think of them than the God of the universe. This is the mistake we all make until we realize that really nobody is necessarily concerned about us. For some of us, it takes going through a major life event to find out who our real friends and family are.

The people who will support you when you are going through the cutting process are the actual people that God has placed to help lead you through the change. If you find that you are around an entirely new association of friends and maybe no family, that is okay, too. Eventually, you will be able to return to the ones who held you in your sin and shame. But not until you are strong and rooted in your faith. You will be the one to go back and show them what it looks like to transform into the version that God had intended you to be before sin and shame got a hold of your mind. God hand-picks people to lead and guide you through your transformation.

Once you cut out the input and association that was causing your sin and illness, you will feel empty. Like a puzzle that only has the outer part built, and the rest of the puzzle is missing. You will feel empty and alone. It is important during this time to allow the Holy Spirit to fill up that space.

> *In him you were also circumcised with a circumcision not performed by human hands. Your whole self ruled by the flesh was put off when you were circumcised by Christ, having been buried with him in baptism, in which you were also raised with him through your faith in the working of God, who raised him from the dead. When you were dead in your sins and in the uncircumcision of your flesh, God made you alive with Christ. He forgave us all our sins, having canceled the charge of our legal indebtedness, which stood against us and condemned us; he has taken it away, nailing it to the cross. And having disarmed the*

> *powers and authorities, he made a public spectacle of them, triumphing over them by the cross.*
>
> COLOSSIANS 2:11-15

Here, Paul is explaining circumcision in Christ to the Colossians. Circumcision raises you from the dead (just as Christ was raised from the dead) by making you alive in Christ; by forgiving our sins and canceling our debt, Jesus took away our guilt, sin, and shame and nailed it to the cross…He was publicly humiliated for us. He carries our sin, guilt, and shame now so we can be free to live in love. We are no longer accusing but refusing to hinder peace, love, joy, and happiness no matter the circumstances because we know who is in control of our future.

In Romans 3, a question is posed: what value is there in circumcision? And the answer is much in every way. Number one, when God circumcises you, He is entrusting you with the very words that are His. The God of the universe cares so much about you that He will give you His own words so that when you speak, your words will be proved right. You are also circumcised so that you can discern or judge between good and evil. When you have the spirit within you, God's words are in you, and that is how you will know who speaks from His word or from the world's word.

When we cut out sin and are washed in the blood of Christ and cleansed with His righteousness, we can then repent, and our thinking becomes cleansed with the words of God. It is through the reading and hearing of God's words that we are cleansed. We can't be trusted with the truth until we are aware of our sin; it must be cut away for us. Surgery is necessary, painful but necessary.

I believe that when you have a desire to read the Bible and can't understand it, it is because you have not cut sin out yet. You must have a genuine heart to change. Only God knows when you are truly ready to make that change. Jesus will come knocking. You will feel an inner pull toward perfection. Jesus, our savior, healer, redeemer, our word…He changes us. You are going to feel stuck in a circumstance until you decide to make the decision for circumcision. You can either stay at a stance, or you can cut away sin from your life, undergo the pain of surgery, and then work toward recovery.

Jesus started His ministry with Jewish men; these men were already in an original covenant with God. These original twelve disciples did not need to be circumcised because their parents, grandparents, and all the way to Abraham were in covenant with God, just like they are today. These individuals still practice circumcising their male children at the age of eight days. Not all people start with DNA that is in covenant with God. The original twelve were sent among the Gentiles to spread the word of the gospel. I can only imagine what they had to come up against.

These men were literally changing the physical appearance of men. The men who went through circumcision as grown adults had to expose themselves to another man. Trust another man with his livelihood, his future. If this went wrong, there was a possibility of no more children, especially at that time with the threat of an infection. They had to be willing to completely alter their appearance, to change the way they looked, and to leave a permanent scar. Now you are not the "same" as the others around you…you are different. You have gone from being one way and fitting in with one group, your family, your friends, who have known you since birth…and left them to follow Christ. Now you are different, and others will notice, and they will be mean.

Make a stand. John 15:18–19: "If the world hates you, keep in mind it hated me first. If you belonged to the world, it would love you as its own. As it is, you do not belong to the world, but I have chosen you out of the world. That is why the world hates you." Jesus' own words explain why you may feel hatred. At some point, we have to say we're going to be willing to stand on principle, to change, to get cut, to believe in Jesus. Once these men made the choice and proved their loyalty to Jesus, they were given the power of the Holy Spirit and were able to change and impact people everywhere they went for the rest of their lives.

It takes twelve individuals to make us up, essentially. We are the DNA of our mom and dad, and they are the DNA of their parents. Altogether, that makes up twelve individuals. How, you may be asking? Our mom and dad are both products of their parents, who were made up of and raised by their parents. You do not count your parents because they made us. We are a product of what made them... So, their parents and grandparents, who are twelve individuals. These twelve individuals shaped our parents, and they shaped us. The reason why this is important is because who you are will affect not only your children but also your grandchildren and their children. We are a direct product of how our parents were raised, and we have no say in where we are planted.

God hand-selects out our family and our lineage. Each and every one of us has a specific time, day, month, and year that we were born. It matters. You matter. The moment you were born, the earth took notice, and something shifted. Your place counts. You are not just another number. You are not an average person. You are a chosen child of God. God has a story for you to tell. Your family tree has value and purpose, and so do you. You are going to break the chains of the ones who came before you and create a wave of power in the Holy Spirit. The surgery that must occur in order for us to break away from our DNA and begin our new life *in Christ* is painful. We may leave behind people we love, but God will care and guide them just like He did you. He will never leave or forsake any of us. We are the ones who leave Him; He never turns His back on us. Will you choose Him? Will you make the decision for circumcision? Will you stand for His mission?

CHAPTER 11:

Recovered

Recovered. When you look it up in the dictionary, it will tell you that it means to get back, regain. To recover is to bring back into a normal position, to make up for, to find or identify again. Recover is what God did to Adam and Eve when He went to seek them out for their morning walk after they had fallen into sin. When He looked for them, they were covered up with "fig" leaves and hiding. When I thought about the word "fig," I thought about other words that start with "fig," and they are both affected when we eat from the tree of "knowledge of good and evil:" they are "fight" and "figure."

The only reason why we fight with one another is to determine who is "right or wrong," so it makes sense that the "fig" tree is what they covered their "figures" up with. If you eat or consume food that is not good for your body, then your figure is going to be covered with the things that you are consuming.

What is fat if not a cover over your figure? The original figure that God has intended for you is not overweight, yet most of us are overweight nowadays. Gluttony is a sin, and food was my personal sin. I was "cuffed to cake..." thanks to Pastor Todd for that brilliant sermon. I knew that food was where I turned during times of need, desire, want, hurt, pain, and loneliness. The problem I had with food began the moment I was born, and I still have food challenges to this very day. If there is one lesson I have learned in life, it is that we are what we *consume*. We are what we are "conned into summing" (Trevor Baker) each and every day. As one of our mentors always says. John 4:34: "'My food,' said Jesus, 'is to do the will of him who sent me and to finish his work.'" So is ours; the bread of life is the food we consume to finish His work now.

All the way back to Adam and Eve, food has been a source of problems for man and wife. Just ask any couple how they get along when they are trying to decide where to go out to dinner for a date night. I think every couple has a deep level of PTSD from our original ancestors, Adam and Eve, since original sin started with dinner.

We all start out in different home settings. We all grow up differently and in different cultures. Our culture determines the type of food we consume. The way we eat is passed down from generation to generation. The way we consume from everywhere is determined by our parents and their parents. I'm no different, and neither are you. We are built of the tree we come from. In the Bible, Matthew 7:16 says, "By their fruit you will recognize them. Do people pick grapes from thornbushes, or figs from thistles?" You are a "fighter," are you not? You are what you consume. This was a harsh truth that I would be coming up against in the coming months and even years.

The reality is that when we all accept Christ as our Lord and Savior, that is the exact time the enemy is going to come and try to snatch you away from the blessings that God has in store for you. The second you start taking your commitment to God seriously and start to prune away the things that are holding you back from walking the path that God has for you, the enemy will come along to steal, kill, and destroy all of your dreams and ambitions. He will remind you where you came from. He will remind you of who you came from and what you were born into. But God! You are no longer bound by the stones that have been weighing you down. The life you were born into is not the life that God has for you. God has a chosen life, one that you can not even imagine. It is so much more abundant than you could ever imagine. But will you trust Him? Will you allow yourself to go through the pain of the recovery process?

The process of recovery started multiple times for me during the last five years, as I have been undergoing surgery after surgery. Each and every one of those surgeries started with a cut from a scalpel blade and was left with a scar. There was a lesson learned from each and every wound that I endured. Jesus will take our sin and turn it into a "son," a lesson. I am a little slow, and it took me a long time to learn, but if we do not listen to God, then we will end up turning to sin, and then the Son will have to come and clean up our lives, but He is so graceful, that He will leave us with a lasting lesson to teach others.

In the garden, Adam and Eve were living the perfect life. They had everything they ever could have wanted. God was providing them with everything, and they still chose to sin, and so do we. The sin of Adam and Eve started what every human has had to endure until the return of Jesus. The first parents of this world failed. And so did yours. And so will you. We all do. We all fail to be perfect. We all fail not to eat off of the tree of "knowledge of good and evil." We are all human and question "why?" all the time. So here we all end up naked in our own garden. Covered with "fig" leaves. We don't recognize ourselves because we have drifted so far off of what God originally intended for us to be because we chose to be blind to the reality of our lives. We started to pick off every other tree around us and not focus on our own trees.

Will you face God in your garden? When do you feel the call of God? Do you hear Him calling for you in your nakedness? He wants to recover you. He wants to spend the time nursing your wounds. He wants to meet you in the garden and help you to till the dirt and remove the weeds. He wants to help start the process of recovery.

To recover is to change the covering of something, from our outer appearance to the covering of our heart. When we sin, just like Adam and Eve in the garden, we feel it deep inside of us, and we feel afraid; we want to cover up the sin or ourselves. When we sin and become aware of the possible consequences of the sin, we start to either run away or fight it out. We all have the same instinct when we feel like we are in danger: we "fight or flight."

In Genesis 3:7, once they ate the fruit, "Then the eyes of both of them were opened, and they realized they were naked; so they sewed fig leaves together and made coverings for themselves."

What does a couple sew once they sin? Fights! That is what they sew. They start stringing together one fight after another. Until we have a string of "fig leaves" and have made an entirely new wardrobe to cover up the huge figures we have created by shoving more and more sin down each other's throats. We do not listen to each other, and we certainly are not stopping to listen to anything God has to say. Listen when you sin, because God is calling you. He is asking you, "Where are you?" (Genesis 3:9).

In the last five years, I have recovered from six surgeries and even more hospital stays…viruses, bacterial infections, and many, many other things. Each and every one of those times, I spent time asking God, "What am I supposed to learn from this?" Did I ask why? Yes. Did I ask when? Yes. Did I ask how? Yes. Did I ask what? Yes. Did I ask who? Yes. I have questioned God more in the last five years than the entirety of the prior forty-three, but I have never questioned if He was with me.

Deep down inside, I do not think there is one living, breathing creature that questions the existence of our creator. There is but *one*, and He is all-knowing, being, seeing, doing, hearing. He touches each and every one of us each and every second of every day. We may question His existence, but He never questions ours. There is nothing you can ever do or say that will surprise Him. He knows your every thought and feeling. So, just open up to Him. Stop running. Stop covering up. Stop covering up who you are from the one who created you. He wants you to know Him. He knows you. Do you want to get to know Him? Or will you keep running?

Maybe you are reading this thinking, *if God knows everything, then why do I need to change who*

I am? He knows who we are, so He knows why we behave a certain way. He forgives everyone, right? So why can't we just live our life? If God created me, then He knows why I need to behave a certain way. Who is my sin hurting? What if my sin only hurts me? I am not hurting anyone else, so if God sees and knows me, then He gets why I have to behave a certain way to get through the day. Right?

When Adam and Eve sinned in the garden, God did recover them. He made garments of skin for Adam and Eve. Therefore, their sin caused death. The death of the animal that had to be sacrificed to make the clothing they would need because God was going to reward them. Reward…not with coins, land, treasures, a kingdom. They were about to be rewarded with a new location. God had to prepare them for the place they would be rewarded with. Just like He will prepare you and me for the places that He will reward us with.

God is also going to prepare you for the reward that you will be receiving. First, though, we need to talk about what the recovery process looks like. This is a different length of time for each individual. Since this is a story about what has been revealed to me through the Holy Spirit, I will reveal how the Holy Spirit has been speaking to me through the long process of recovery that I have been growing through.

The most important thing when you start a recovery process is to make sure that you are following in the footsteps of a mentor. Jesus is our mentor. He has traveled before you and is paving a way for you, but it is up to us to follow Him to where He is leading us.

I remember the exact moment that I started to "cover up" and not be who God made me to be. We moved from one school district to another in the summer of (I am going to age myself) 1988. My sister graduated from High School, and this seemed like the perfect time to switch me from one school to the other. I had been doing research all throughout the seventh grade, so I was ready for summer break. I knew that my dad would buy me anything I asked for because he was "rich" (or so I assumed at the time). All seventh grade, I observed how the "cool" or "popular" kids acted and what they wore. How they all talked and behaved. I knew we were moving, and I was planning on ditching the dorky clothes and being a whole new person. Everyone at my last school knew me as a "church girl," and this was not going to be the case at my new school. I was going to change. I was determined to change, and that is exactly what I did.

My parents became very preoccupied with their own lives and struggles, and I started to sin in every single way I could. I was doing everything that I should not be doing, and nobody seemed to care. My parents went out most of the evenings, and I was left to do whatever I pleased from the age of thirteen on, and I did. I started smoking, drinking, and having sex at fourteen years old. My house had pornography in it from the age of five until I moved out and lived on my own. There were Playboy magazines in every bathroom and all around. My stepdad loved women. He was not disrespectful to women, though…he loved women, beautiful women, so I believed that in order to be loved, I needed to behave the same way the women in those magazines behaved.

Music, drugs, alcohol, sex, friends, and then, if someone noticed, school. This was my life from age fourteen to eighteen until I dropped out of high school. I ditched all of tenth grade, and my parents had no idea. This was the start of me not liking authority. I believed that I had the right to control my own life, and nobody else seemed to care. My sin started at fourteen years old. That behavior continued off and on until someone showed me how to live through my values. They showed me what it looked like to be covered in the blood of Jesus. To not see myself through what I was doing, but who I was, who I am, and who God created me to be. God does not look at us and see our failures. He sees our hearts. He sees the things we do not, the things we desperately wish to see, but only God has the eyes to see.

I wandered for forty years, thinking I was living a life following Jesus. I was only following my own selfish ambitions. I can see that now that God has cut away the things that were holding me back. God will break those things He wants to divide and spread amongst His sheep. When the people were hungry while Jesus was preaching, He took bread, He broke it, and then He divided it. I believe that if you feel like you are being broken, it is because God can take pieces of you and spread them, leaving a piece of Himself behind in a memory that is meant to be a representation of Him.

The Lord showed me an example of a cover-up that I am so guilty of, and that is simply "covering up my roots." Of course, I am referring to my hair. I started to grow gray hair…one here and one there, at around eighteen years old. In my late thirties, though, the gray hair started to take over, and I made the decision that I wanted to "cover up" my gray roots. This is no different than what we do on a day-to-day basis with our lives. We live a life that is not one we are proud of, and then we spend money and energy covering up the root of the problem.

The gray hair is not gone…it is simply "covered," "disguised," and not a true representation of who we really are. Do you tell everyone you meet, "Hi! I have gray hair under this dye"? No, of course not. But you are also not presenting a true representation of who you really are. This is just one of many examples of how we cover up who and what we truly are so that we can keep our true roots hidden. What are you covering up that you want to reveal to God?

Credit is another *huge* way we cover up who

we really are. Let's face it: we can not afford the "things" we have, and that is why we borrow from our future to pay for our present. The issue is that you, then, are trying to write a future for you that only God knows the path for. You are essentially writing checks that you have no idea if you will ever be able to pay back or not. We oftentimes care more about how we "look" to those around us than how we actually are. We cover up our insecurities with new clothes, cars, homes, and gadgets, and we place unnecessary pressure on ourselves. It is not only unnecessary pressure, but it is also not God-given pressure; it is a pressure that you have placed upon yourself. This type of pressure will never grow you; it will only ever crush you. God will never put on you more than you can handle; however, your choices will place such a heavy burden on you that you will not be able to lift off the burden until you call upon God to lift the burden off of you.

Another example of recovery in our lives is just how we progress through natural growth and development processes. We start in complete dependence on our parents. We are confined to only where we can shimmy to, squirm to, or be carried by another to. We would not last more than a few days if someone did not care for us. But we go from being covered with diapers and surrounded by bars (crib) to running to a bathroom, wearing underwear, and buckling ourselves into the backseat of the car. This goes on and on throughout our lives…but it takes at least sixteen years before someone hands you the keys to a moving vehicle. Or before you are able to travel out of state in that vehicle. The majority of us have traveled this path of recovery. Each time we are recovered our soul (our covering), our mind, will, and emotions change.

I will never forget the day I put on my official uniform, the day I was a registered nurse. The first day that I was going to walk into a hospital as a registered nurse and be assigned my own patient to be responsible for their life. I will never forget the responsibility I felt. The truth is…I was not responsible for anyone but myself. I, however, did not take my responsibility that way. I started to let the weight of responsibility crush me and my covering…my soul, my mind, will, and emotions. This is when the crushing would begin to my ignorance. I stopped attending church on Sunday and started going to the hospital on Sunday; after all, the people needed me to help save them. I was not saving anyone. I was destroying my soul, and unfortunately, the longer your soul is crushed, the deeper the sin becomes rooted, and eventually, it will reach your container, and your body will start to show signs of the crushing of your soul. But God has so much mercy on us that He will not allow one of His children to be lost. He will come after you if you wander away from the herd, if you wander out of listening distance.

In Genesis 3:9, Adam heard, and he was afraid. When we are living in sin, the enemy will use the things we hear to cause fear in us. The enemy knows that even if we hear, we will fear now that our eyes are opened. Prior to our sin, or knowledge of sin, we were innocent. We had no idea sin was a thing. We are actually responsible, once we know about sin, to stop sinning. Until we are aware of sin, we are considered innocent and immature. There are innocent people in every part of the world, in and out of churches each and every day. We only hide because we are aware of our sin. People who are living out in the open, just sinning away in the daylight, on the streets...it is because they are unaware of their sin. Once we start to hide our sin, though...very few people are ever found again.

Many people become aware of their sin, and instead of running to God and asking for forgiveness, they hide and cover up. We ignore the issue. Bury our sins, our iniquities, our infirmities. We add layer over layer of covering until one day, we just don't even recognize us. We have become lost. Fear is a natural human response; it is what and who we turn to during our time of fear that is important. As soon as we realize we have sinned, we are to go straight to God and admit our mistake. God will recover us if we come to Him with our sin. We fear being "caught" doing something wrong, but when we fail, who do we expect to "fix" the problem? When we use our own mind, will, and intentions to solve life problems, we get our results. But when we allow our choices to be led by a set of standards set in place by God, modeled by Jesus, and led in us through the Holy Spirit, then we will get the results that God has for us. His will then can be done on earth as it is in heaven.

We cover up in shame when we take the stand of

guilt. When we fall into sin or even watch another fall into sin, we pick a side. We pick the side of the victim or victor at every sin encounter, whether it is our sin or another's. Our mind does not differentiate between real and fiction. Our emotions feel the pain of sin, if it is ours or another's. This is why we should avoid sin at all costs. Run from it. If we are exposed, we are to immediately run to God. If you are filled with the Holy Spirit, you will be convicted that this is sin and to turn away, and immediately speak to the Father regarding the situation.

Adam and Eve did not run to God when they sinned. They covered up their sin. Never cover sin. Always confess. Immediately confess sin. We Christians should never be ashamed to confess when we mess up because we do not ever carry our sin. We hang it on the line like a piece of laundry that just got cleaned, old-school style. Anytime we fall into sin, we run to the Father, and Jesus washes us clean and hangs our sin out to dry. We are then able to return to ourselves…we are washed by the blood of Jesus. He washes us clean and renews us each and every day. We are clothed in the righteousness of Jesus. Come to the Father naked and allow Him to recover you in the righteousness of Jesus Christ.

"I will clothe his enemies with shame" (Psalm 132:18). Whether we realize it or not…if we are overweight, it is because we are covered in shame. Because when we are bad or feel bad, we Americans eat. A lot of the time it is that we "see" shameful things, we feel "shame" for others, and we eat because we can't separate ourselves from being an eyewitness and being guilty. We don't go to God and ask for forgiveness for watching shameful content/news/movies, whatever…so we cover up in shame. When most of us are not even guilty of anything but "seeing" falsehoods or an eyewitness account, which is not even accurate, but unfortunately, our minds do not know how to separate falsehoods from reality or truth. If you do not know the Truth (Holy Spirit), then you will spend all day, every day, searching for the Truth, picking from the tree of "knowledge of good and evil."

When God is making a move in our lives, we often change into new clothing or have to wear a new uniform. Once you make any team, you change into the uniform, and God's team is no different. We all put on the clothing of Jesus' righteousness once we accept that He is Our Lord and Savior. I think that a lot of us believe that when we are baptized with a water baptismal, this is what reclothes us. But in fact, it is not us knowing we are saved, but us seeing that we were in dirty rags, and that we are in need of cleansing. When we see our need, this is when the power of the Holy Spirit starts to take over, and then our God will turn up the heat and purify us so that He can recover us in His righteousness, and then we can receive the reward that He has for us. We must be fully recovered before we can receive our reward.

CHAPTER 12:

Reward

I started with the beginning, so does that mean that this is the *end*? I started with my first encounter that I remember with God, my creator. I always knew I was created by God. Then, at age seven, I accepted Jesus as my friend. I was not old enough to understand anything about the Holy Spirit, but I could feel the presence of someone around me all the time. Even though I spent the majority of my days and nights alone, I never felt as if I was truly alone until I was facing the first pain that could not be fixed by anyone or anything in this world. It was then and only then did I realize how far off course I had drifted. I was not headed toward heaven. I was not even pointed in the right direction. The only thing that saved me was the fact that even though I was not paying attention to God, He was paying attention to me. He rewarded me the moment he placed me in a new association of people. The blessing will always come from someone else. The power will always be passed from one person to another. Jesus must be introduced to you, and you must hear His story, accept it, and ask Him to come into your heart and heal you.

I am reminded of stories in the Bible where Peter introduced his mother-in-law to Jesus, and she was instantly healed and started to serve Him, and her family. Or the four who lowered their friend on a mat through a roof to get their friend to Jesus for healing. It is our responsibility to introduce people to Jesus as believers and followers to our friends, family, and anyone we meet so they, too, can experience the healing that Jesus has for each and every one of us.

The word reward in the dictionary (Merriam-Webster) is something that is given in return for good or evil done or received that is offered or given for some service or attainment. "Re-" means again, anew, back, or backward, and "-ward" means that moves, tends, faces, or is directed toward. Therefore, to be rewarded is to be turned back toward a specific direction. Let's face it: to be rewarded is to point in the direction of our heavenly Father. My goal with writing this book is to point some of my friends, family, acquaintances, and even strangers toward the direction of our heavenly Father.

A reward is not some monetary gain or trinket that you get to keep. There is no great thing that you will get as a reward. Jesus says in Revelation 22:12–13, "Look, I am coming soon! My reward is with me, and I will give to each person according to what they have done. I am the Alpha and the Omega, the First and the Last, the Beginning and the End." The reward comes with Jesus. He is the Beginning and the End. While writing this book, I started to think about the end. The end is where He is. The question is, have we been purified enough to enter into the house of God?

I heard a gentleman ask once that if you were to die today and show up at God's house and knock, would He know who you are? Would He let you into His home? He would only consider it if you knew His Son, Jesus Christ. "No one who denies the Son has the Father; whoever acknowledges the Son has the Father also" (1 John 2:23). So, your relationship with the Son is the beginning, and in order to get into God's house and get the ultimate reward, which is to live in His home with Him, you must have Jesus, the end.

Jesus will come knocking on each of our doors and ask to be let in. He called me out of darkness and into the light. Just like many of you, I was a lost sheep. I had wandered away from the path that Jesus had laid out before me. I was knocked off track. Jesus says He did not come to save the righteous but the sinner. I was a sinner. Maybe you come from the belief that once a sinner, always a sinner, and that Jesus covers all sin. However, in the Bible I read, it does not say that. "Everyone who sins breaks the law; in fact, sin is lawlessness. But you know that he appeared so that he might take away our sins. And in him is no sin. No one who lives in him keeps on sinning. No one who continues to sin has either seen him or known him" (1 John 3:4–6). If you continue to sin, you are not living in Him. Jesus comes to take away sin, remove it, and free you from it. If you choose to keep on sinning, it is because you have not purified yourself with the heart and mind of Jesus. You must purify yourself. Wash out the old and renew yourself with Jesus. "Blessed are those who wash their robes, that they may have the right to the tree of life and may go through the gates into the city" (Revelation 22:14).

Sin, the word, when broken down, means "labeling within." S- is the Latin symbol for label, and -in is within. So, anytime we label ourselves anything that is "worldly," we are adding titles to ourselves that God did not give us. The ultimate sin is taking worldly labels and placing them on people and us. If I were to label myself with some of those titles, for example, I may say: I am a Sagittarius, introverted, type A, loner, nurse, etc. The list can go on and on. But nowhere in the Bible does God use any of those terms to label me or you. I was very guilty of applying labels to people…he is an alcoholic, a drug abuser, a lawyer, a cheater. These may be things a person has done, but these are not labels that we keep. If you follow Jesus, then you know that He comes to take all the sins/labels away from us and transforms us into Himself. This takes a willingness to partner with Him, to enter into a covenant with Him.

Of course, once you are called and enter into a covenant, you must be cut. You must choose to cut the things out of your life that do not serve your future. You cannot drag around a 100-pound knapsack of bad choices and decisions that you have made your entire life. Let Jesus take away your burdens and carry them off, along with all the titles and sins you have placed on you. It is up to you to start to cut away the things that do not align with God's purpose for you.

I am not saying that I have all the answers; God knows I do not. I am in constant progression to be more like Christ each and every day. I am still pruning away all of the things that are not serving my future. The goal is to become so light that the long, narrow road that must be traveled to enter into His kingdom will not seem so long or lonely.

We all are infected by our input and association. It is also up to us to make sure that we are irrigating and aspirating the input and association that is not breathing life into us. Jesus came and defeated death, hell, and the grave, and I will not continue to speak of death, hell, or the grave over anyone. My husband recently passed away, and although my life has been completely changed and my heart torn in two, I know that he is not dead, in hell, or in a grave. He is living with Jesus, and he has been rewarded, and his reward is based solely on what he has done. Jesus is the only one who knows our hearts and minds, and that is what He will judge. Not our actions but what is in our hearts and minds.

Not everyone will have to go through seven major surgeries and the loss of a spouse to be rewarded. But we will have to go through a process of purifying ourselves if we want to have the right to the tree of life and enter through the gates into the city. "Outside are the dogs, those who practice magic arts, the sexually immoral, the murderers, the idolaters, and everyone who loves and practices falsehood" (Revelation 22:15). I believe in angels, even today. An angel is a messenger for God, someone who comes with a message from our heavenly Father. I believe that the things I have been through have placed me as a messenger for God. I am simply here to tell you that what you have heard your whole life…may not be accurate, and I want to help as many people enter the city as possible. Friends, you must purify yourself.

When thinking about a title for this book, I chose *The Endgin* because Jesus is the end, and gin is an alcohol that goes through a rigorous purification process, just like myself. No, one dip in a river did not purify me. One baptismal did not wash away my sins. It took month after month, cut after cut, and even the loss of my spouse to show me what it actually takes to be rewarded. To be pointed in the direction of the king. I do not want to get to the end of this life and be told I must stay outside with the "dogs." I also do not want that for any of you.

Jesus is calling you. He wants to take away all the sin in your life, each and every worldly label that you have placed on yourself. He wants to give you access to the tree of life. He wants to reward you. Friends, all it takes is for you to believe that He Is the Son of Man and the Son of God. Just like you were made from your mom and dad, He too was conceived of His mother and His Father. He was 100 percent human and 100 percent God. He is the *way*, the *truth*, and the *life*, and no one can enter His Father's gate and into the city without Him.

I pray for each and every one who reads this that my story will encourage and help you to know that God loves you. That God created you. God knitted you together. He knows each and every cell in your body. God hears you. God listens to each word you say. God has been with you since the beginning, and He will be with you till the end. He is the beginning, and He is the end. I will spend the rest of my days pointing people toward the direction of Jesus. He loves you, and so do I.

THE ENDGIN.

Printed in the USA
CPSIA information can be obtained
at www.ICGtesting.com
LVHW021156041224
798233LV00004B/126